THE COLD COUNTRY

Susan Hill

The Cold Country

and other plays for radio

British Broadcasting Corporation

Published by the
British Broadcasting Corporation,
35 Marylebone High Street,
London W1M 4AA
ISBN 0 563 12827 5
First published 1975
© Susan Hill 1975
Printed in England by
Silver End Press Ltd, Silver End, Witham, Essex CM8 3QD

Contents

FOR GUY VAESEN

Introduction

I was born in 1942, and mine was a generation of radio listeners. I did not see a television programme until 1953 (the Coronation), and my family did not own a set until the year I left home for University. These are facts, not proud claims from a member of the anti-television lobby. But for most writers, the better habits of a lifetime are laid down, and the imaginative influences which bear fruit in later years most strongly exerted, in childhood and adolescence.

An enormous number of factors go into the making of a novelist; I can identify some – growing up as the only child of older parents in an isolated northern seaside resort, learning to read very early and subsequently devouring books of widely varying content and quality, but in huge quantities. Other factors remain mysterious. But although I began as a radio dramatist some twelve years after writing my first novel, the step was not so much a forwards one, in a new and unfamiliar direction, as a 'backwards' one. I was returning to a medium not so much with as *in* which I grew up. Radio was in my blood, as television and the cinema have never been (which is why, on the few occasions I have worked in those media, I have found the going so hard). Certainly, the writing of radio plays is a challenge and an excitement, and I encounter new difficulties, as well as problems, with every piece. But I slipped into the medium as into an old glove, which seemed to have moulded itself long ago to the shape of my own hand, and I am still surprised that I did not make use of it much earlier.

Inevitably, the radio programmes to which I listened when young were as varied in subject-matter and quality as the books I read, and my experience of drama began with the Toytown plays and serial adaptations of 'Children's Hour'. There were some restrictions on the number of listening-hours I was allowed to put in, but although some programmes might be considered 'too late at night' for me to hear, there was no nonsense talked about any being 'too old' for me. (I read many books which made the deepest impression upon me, long before I might have been considered 'old enough' to understand them.)

I heard hundreds of radio plays and the majority, good as well as mediocre, passed in one ear and out of the other; only three remain vividly in my memory now. Two are classics of radio writing, and I have become more closely familiar with them, through repeated readings and hearings, in adulthood. But it was the first occasion of listening to them which stayed with me. I remember my own imaginative response – the world I created within me, to match the dialogue and sound-pictures, the faces I put to the voices of the characters. The initial experience of any work of art which is to prove increasingly significant for the rest of one's life seems always to be surrounded in memory, like a fly in amber, by highly personal, incidental details; so that I recall, for example, the pattern of the upholstery on the chair in which I was sitting, the contents of the sandwich I was eating, when I first heard *Under Milk Wood*, and Louis Mac-Neice's *The Dark Tower*. Moreover, a true response to any product of the creative imagination is a more individual matter than simple recognition of, and admiration for, the universally acclaimed masterpieces – which may be no more than an attitude of deference. One radio play which made not only an immediate impact upon me, as a young listener, but which has had a strong influence on my own work, was a Third Programme adaptation of Marghanita Laski's *Little Boy Lost*, starring Margaret Rawlings and produced in 1957. (I heard it only once and, unlike the Thomas and MacNeice plays, have never read any scripted version.)

I began to 'write' (in the sense of making up characters and weaving stories around them) almost before I learned to read, and my initial literary excursions were all dramatic. I made up puppet plays, epics for a cardboard toy theatre, nursery dramas – all parts acted aloud by me, and with dialogue and (scanty) plot improvised as I went along. But when I began to write seriously, I wrote prose – stories, and very soon, a novel. Plays became childish things, which I was anxious to put away when I aspired to be adult. It took someone else to lead me back into that early world of drama. I began my career as a radio playwright by a series of what, at the time, seemed mere chances and coincidences, but which, with hindsight, reveal themselves as one more pattern of divine guidance. Two novels of mine were adapted, with great skill, by Guy Vaesen, as plays for transmission on Radio 4, but my next book, *I'm the King of the Castle*, was unsuitable for translation to the air in dramatic form, and Guy (then a Senior Radio Drama Producer) suggested I write an original radio play. I was doubtful about the idea, but began work on 'The End of Summer' the following week. It was a piece which wrote itself. At the time, I thought I was playing very safe by restricting myself to a length of sixty minutes, and to two main characters. In fact, this can be the most difficult format of all to follow; any faults stick out like sore thumbs, flagging invention and unconvincing dialogue are not glossed over, and the listener's attention held by the use of music, an assorted battery of sound effects, and a 'cast of thousands'.

'The End of Summer' is a beginner's piece, and its flaws are obvious to me now. Nevertheless, it does contain all the elements of which I was to make greater use in subsequent plays. There is music, and it is not merely incidental; the Schubert song, 'Frühlingstraum', is a leitmotif, and its words stimulate

8

reactions, emotions and changes in the two characters, all of which are reflected in their conversation.

In the second volume of his autobiography, *At Home*, the late William Plomer noted that all writers have 'some unusual concentration of interest, some fantasy or obsession or predilection which has been an essential motive force in their work. It may be a passion for a person, place or thing. . . .' Some of my own obsessions have been transitory, and I have worked them out, as basic themes or images, in a single book, story or play. Others are permanent, and I return to them, to find further inspiration. But I have never written anything which has not reflected one, or several, of these passions – they are far more than mere 'interests'. At the time of writing 'The End of Summer' I was obsessed with the moon; ever since I sat in the garden of a remote Dorset cottage listening to the transmitted voices of the first men on the moon and looking, simultaneously, at the real moon in the sky, poetic, mythical and musical moon-associations had danced through my head. The moon has always been linked in men's minds – and hence, in their legends, superstitions and art – with water, and although my moon-infatuation proved temporary, my obsession with water, in all its forms, and with ideas of death by drowning is permanent. A psychoanalyst might make much – or little – of it; in either case, it is dangerous for an artist to delve too deeply into the sources of his principle fantasies, and the reasons underlying them.

Each of the radio plays in this volume deals with one, or more, of my passions. The absorption in young children, about whom I write constantly, was greatly stimulated by the Marghanita Laski play.

After 'The End of Summer' I had more ambitious ideas. 'Lizard in the Grass' developed one of my water-obsessions – the image of sunken and lost cities, whether fabulous (Atlantis, Avalon) or real. I had frequently walked along the cliffs above Dunwich, in Suffolk, imagining that once great and prosperous city and its inhabitants, long ago lost beneath the North Sea, and always half-expecting to hear the legendary sounding of church bells from the deep. Plays, like novels and stories, are formed by a process of accretion; ideas floating around in the writer's mind (or in odd notebooks) gradually come together. I went to a convent school on the East coast, and I was as rebellious and dreamy as the heroine Jane of 'Lizard in the Grass'. I transferred my convent to the Dunwich cliffs, and then had two elements of a play. Since reading English at University, I had been intermittently fascinated by the work, character and certain events in the life of the sixteenth-century poet John Skelton. But it was a chance rereading of an essay about him by E. M. Forster (in his collection entitled *Two Cheers for Democracy*), while I was mulling over the possible new play, which provided me with the final and most important element. Forster's essay, a masterly piece of evocation and analysis, led me to other books about Skelton, but I took great liberties with him, mainly by removing him from the inland town of Diss, in Norfolk, where he was Rector, and setting him down at Dunwich, at the time of the great storm which washed the town away. I also brought him into 'the present' by making him materialise from one of his bones, which Jane finds on Dunwich beach. I was learning that, in radio drama, one can do anything at all with the juxtaposition of events in time and space. 'Lizard in the Grass' was not so much a difficult play to write as to organise – rather like fitting together a four-dimensional jigsaw.

There is a long and honourable tradition in radio drama of the use of specially composed music, and this was the first play in which Geoffrey Burgon collaborated with me, and with the producer, Guy Vaesen, to produce a setting of some lines of Skelton, for boy's treble voice and harp (a magical soundcom bination).

I had now written two quite distinct types of radio play. The small-cast, closed-circle kind, with minimal sound effects. And the multi-stranded, many-layered piece. I find that a dramatic idea fits, from the very beginning, into one or the other form, that each presents its own particular challenges, possibilities and problems, and that the radio medium can take both in its stride.

Ever since my imagination was fired by the accounts of the ascent of Everest, in 1953, I have been spasmodically obsessed with the cold, white, desolate worlds of the Arctic and the Antarctic, but I was not planning a radio play as I listened to Vaughan Williams's *Sinfonia Antarctica* one evening in 1970. However, ideas drop down from heaven, and clamour to be made immediate use of, and before the music was over I had been presented with four male characters (ready equipped with names) in a hopeless situation, stranded in a tent in a blizzard at the dead-end of some expedition. 'The Cold Country' is another closed-circle play (though there is some rather clumsy use of flashback). This was one of the few occasions when I sat down to write and followed my nose; the theme and ideas unfolded one by one, as I began to wonder *why* men went on such forays, and to consider what tensions and conflicts the claustrophobic situation of these people would generate. I have often been suspicious of writers who claim that their characters 'take over', because I have always felt very much in control of a given piece of work. Yet in a sense it was Ossie, Chip, Barney and Jo who played out their own drama, and who decided their own fates.

The synopsis, on the basis of which 'Consider the Lilies' was commissioned, hinted at the principal theme and characters – a middle-aged curator of a botanical garden who sees visions, and his relationship with a young, dying girl. But I had not clarified my own ideas sufficiently, and the first version of the play was a disaster; I had taken several wrong turnings, and the dramatic style clashed hopelessly with the inner themes. The final version emerged only after a hard struggle, and it was largely the result of guidance, suggestion and inspiration by Guy Vaesen, so much so that it ought to bear his name, as co-author. I had planned to use specially composed music again; mainly because it was the only way, in a sound medium, that I could suggest the nature of the botanist's visions of dancing angels and the light of God vibrating through plants and trees. But the idea of having two Plant Choruses (one chorus on each stereo speaker) came from Guy Vaesen; and the character of Lesage took on real life and depth and motivation only after he had taken him apart. My original Assistant-curator was a puppet-figure, all bad and black, just as the Curator was all good and white, but such over-simplifications do not have validity outside the structure and world picture of, say, a medieval morality play.

There was more collaboration to come. I had never gone into the studio during the recording of any of my plays; I felt that the presence of the author (even when sitting mute in the background of the control room) would inhibit producer and cast. But I was persuaded to go down for the production of 'Consider the Lilies', only to find that, especially in the final scenes, the actors were having great problems with the interpretation of their parts, because of faulty writing. After long talks with Tony Britton, Helen Worth and, again, Guy Vaesen, several scenes were rearranged, cut, or rewritten entirely in the margins of scripts, during lunch and coffee breaks. I still adhere to my rule that the author must not interfere in any way with the work of producer, actors or technicians, but I shall not be absent from studio during any future recordings, if only because a radio playwright's education is a continuing one, and a day spent listening and observing, in silence, can teach one more than weeks in the study with a script-in-progress.

'Strip Jack Naked' was originally conceived and written as a stage play, which, clearly, it is not, and there were very few alterations needed to fit it for its true medium. It is intended to be a stark piece which must, more than any of the other plays, stand or fall on the basis of its dialogue. The actors have to work extremely hard, there is no music, no use of flashback, sound effects are pared to a minimum, so that the three characters may emerge from cold.

Many people have asked the two questions, 'What can radio drama do? What can't it do?' Whenever I mull over them myself, I return to two quite simple, but comprehensive answers. They are, respectively, 'Anything' and 'Nothing'. Except, of course, for the obvious fact, that radio cannot produce an external visual image, as can the theatre, cinema or television. The visual images must be produced by each individual listener, in his own mind's eye. Radio plays demand the imaginative co-operation of the listener, he participates, he must work as hard, that is, as the conscientious reader of a novel, though he must not be aware that he is 'working'.

Although the audience for radio drama is large, it seems that people are finding it increasingly hard to listen to plays. Education is becoming more than ever dependent upon visual aids, and we live in a world of the fleeting television, cinematic and advertising image, a world in which our eyes are assaulted, whilst we remain passive. We are not being trained *how* to look, our visual awareness is not expanding – rather the reverse. Radio plays demand a patient attentiveness from the listener, but it should also, surely, be an expectant attentiveness. Radio may be, in many ways, a slower-paced medium than television, but the off-button can be depressed with as little effort (it is harder to leave a theatre in mid-act.) The playwright may do anything – except *bore*.

Radio drama is flourishing and expanding, the technical resources available to the playwright are increasing, standards of production can be much higher than in many areas of the modern theatre, and of television, many of our finest actors specifically ask for opportunities to work in radio, because the challenge to them is enormous; if the medium shows up bad writing, perhaps it shows up bad acting even more ruthlessly.

But in the last resort, radio drama is not about technicalities. As a writer, I do not want the audience even to be aware of them, for the moment any of these devices become obtrusive, and the listener asks 'How is it done'? then the play goes out of the window. Plays are about human beings in confrontation – with one another, and with various aspects of their own selves, the contents of their minds and hearts, their pasts, their fears and hopes for the future, the exigencies of their particular situations at given moments in time. When the last word has been said about 'the medium of radio', the most vital words have yet to be spoken; by the writer, through his character, to the listener – person to person. That is all.

S.H.

The End of Summer

The End of Summer was first broadcast on BBC Radio 4, on 26 August 1971, with the following cast.

TOM	*Michael Williams*
SALLY	*Judi Dench*
RESCUE MAN/ANNOUNCER	*Sean Barrett*

The theme music was 'Frühlingstraum' from 'Die Winterreise' by Schubert sung on gramophone records by Peter Pears, accompanied by Benjamin Britten.

Produced by Guy Vaesen

(*Tom is lying in the grass outside the house. It is night. Sally is indoors.*

Sound of wind through tree-tops. Then a sudden scattering of autumn leaves on the terrace)

Tom (*Voice low. Close to us*) It's still there . . . looks exactly the same . . . exactly. It's there and I am here.

(*Wind again*)

(*Tom sighs*) Rain again tonight. Wouldn't be at all surprised. (*Sighs again, contentedly*)

Sally (*Within*) Where are you?

(*Wind. Silence*)

Tom (*Very quietly*) Here. I'm still here.

Sally Tom? Tom?

(*But she is not really wanting to know. Now we are in the room with her*) Never mind. Where . . . Oh lord, look, Eustace, come off that chair . . . not on gramophone records, come off . . . No need to look at me like that. Now you've made it all furry. Soft little hairs between the grooves.

(*Pause. She wipes the record clean*)

Tom (*Close up*) 'Tranquility base . . . are you receiving me? Do you hear me? Tranquility. *Mare tranquilitatis.* Is there any body there? said the Traveller'. . . . Only that stupid little flag, erected and erect, courtesy of the United States of America and florists' wire. (*Imitates voice crackling over radio from the moon*). 'Do you hear me, Houston? Tranquility base. The eagle has landed.' (*Ordinary voice*) No, seriously though, you look exactly the same.

(*Wind again, and then from the house the opening bars of Schubert's 'Frühlingstraum' played on an old, wind-up gramophone*)

(*When he hears it, Tom exclaims softly. Hums to the music. Begins to say the English translation of the words to himself*)

'. . . I dreamed of green meadows, and the happy song of birds. And when . . . .'

(*We move suddenly closer to the singing, and abruptly, at the beginning of the second stanza, the music is taken off*)

Tom (*Sitting up. Loudly*) Hey! What happened? What did you do that for? Sally?

Sally (*From the open door*) What?

Tom The record.

Sally I turned it off. Where are you?

15

Tom Here. (*Grass rustles as he lies down again*) Here.

Sally Where are you? Can't see you . . . can't see anything.

Tom You should.

Sally It's coming out of the house, it makes your eyes go . . . Oh, where are you?

Tom Under the apple tree. (*Sings traditional tune*) 'Who loves to lie with me. And tune his merry note unto the green birds' . . .'

Sally I can't . . .

(*Sally's steps heard through the grass. Tom hums*)

Sally Tom!

Tom Aye, sir!

Sally You're lying in the grass.

Tom I believe I am!

Sally On the ground. You'll get pneumonia.

Tom I have always lain on the grass, on the ground. I have never had pneumonia. *P*-new-moan-yer.

Sally But it was raining. It might rain again.

Tom It will. I can smell it on the wind. And you can hear the river tonight.

Sally You shouldn't lie on the damp grass.

Tom We all sit about too much, in cars and on bar stools and on chairs. I don't like sitting. I have decided that the upright and seated position is entirely unnatural to the human frame. Do you know that? So I lie down on the earth. It isn't really damp.

Sally (*Rustling sound*) Oh. No!

Tom No.

Sally It might seep through.

Tom Have you ever slept all night in front of a log fire? Lying on the floor? I used to do that. My father made log fires. He hated coal, wouldn't have it in the house, he was neurotic about it. So he chopped down trees and piled up the logs and labelled them with little labels – oak, ash, apple, pear. And we had log fires all the winter. I used to look at his hands – they were all hard and calloused in the palms, with chopping the wood. I hated his hands. But I liked the fires. Going to sleep on the floor in front of a crumbling fire. (*Pause*) I suppose it was a sort of therapy. Chopping wood. Gave him a rest from all those mathematical formulae. Some have vegetable gardens. Men like him. Brain men.

Sally Did he lie on the floor in front of his own fires?

Tom Had lumbago. Lumbago for years.

Sally Ah.

Tom I was the one. And like this, out on the grass in summer.

Sally Under the moon.

Tom: 'The moving moon went up the sky,
    And nowhere did abide,
    Softly she was going up,
    And a star or two beside . . .'
        (*Pause*)
    It's still there, isn't it?

Sally Did you think it would have walked away?

Tom Might have. Might have been disgusted. Boom – 'The eagle has landed.' Rape. The rape of Diana. 'Queen and huntress chaste and fair' and then – Then the patter of tiny lunar-module feet. After all those virgin years. All those years, riding high –
'Whenever the moon and stars are out,
    Whenever the wind is high . . .'
Having all that poetry written about you. And then have all that happen. People descending, jumping in you, chucking things about.

Do you know, in India – I read this somewhere in a learned, learned book – in India people used to try and absorb the moon's vital influence by drinking any water in which the luminary is reflected. I think it was India.

Sally You could see the moon in the river.

Tom You can hear the river.

Sally It'll rain again tonight.

Tom Perhaps we'll be stranded here. Marooned on our summer island by the river at flood. Perhaps we'll have to cast lots for who will eat who, to keep alive.

Sally Don't say that!

Tom Why? Why not? Not about the eating, but haven't you liked it here? Of course you have. Don't we plan to stay on and on forever? Haven't you wanted the summer to go on? These nights?

Sally It can't go on. Things don't go on.

Tom We'd be trapped if the river rose.

Sally The summer is over.

Tom A leaf fell on my face.

Sally I don't like water.

Tom You never told me that before. You go down by the river, you walk along the bank. You never said anything about that before.

Sally No.

    (*Sound of her getting up*)

Tom What's the matter?

Sally Damp.

Tom No.

Sally Your father got lumbago.

Tom Lumbago is not caused by the penetration of moisture, it is caused by an inflammation of the muscles surrounding the lumbar vertebrae, brought about by strain.

Sally I hate it. When it rains and you hear the water. I'm afraid.

Tom What's the matter?

Sally The end of it all. The end of summer.

Tom And you turned the music off.

Sally Are you hungry?

Tom Why? Why did you turn the music off?

Sally That music.

Tom That music.

Sally I could make you a bacon sandwich.

Tom Sally?

Sally Eustace sat on the record, did I tell you? His fur was stuck in and out of the grooves, you know? Little white bits of cat fur.

Tom Why?

Sally I don't like to play that now.

Tom You began to.

Sally A mistake.

Tom And then you stopped.

Sally Pneumonia and lumbago would be nasty together.

Tom Don't go.

Sally Or an omelette. I'll do an omelette. There's cheese.

Tom All that night. We stayed up and you played that. All that night. Beneath the moon.

Sally Or a bacon sandwich? You've only to say. It's no trouble.

Tom I sat here and looked up and there it was, there was the moon, not knowing anything about them, getting nearer and nearer, buzzing about her head like bumble bees. (*The voice*) 'Tranquility base. The eagle has landed.' 'Roger, Houston out.' 'It's one small step . . .'

    (*Pause*)

Sally You do go on.

18

Tom And I sat here and there were the voices coming out of the radio, out across this garden, this grass, and there was the moon. 'I see the moon, the moon sees me . . .' God, when was that? I must have been at school. Or somewhere. (*Hums again*) Funny – tunes. You turned that song off.

Sally Oh, for God's sake! (*Tom hums the Schubert tune*) Well, you'd better make up your mind, but I fancy a bacon sandwich.

Tom You change.

Sally Eustace sat on the record. I told you.

Tom The wind is up and the cat goes mad and the river is rising and the moon is unmaidened and (*getting up*) you change, Sally.
    (*Walking up through the grass*)

Sally I wonder if the hedgehog will come?

Tom Put the music on again.

Sally No. It . . .

Tom Put the music on.
    (*Silence. Trees in the wind*)

Sally (*Desperately*) We've been so happy here. All this summer, the days have just gone on and on, haven't they? We've been happy.

Tom And?

Sally Don't you understand anything? Can't you feel?

Tom Nothing.

Sally The leaves falling and – and the end of things.

Tom No! Only of summer. There is always an end to summer.

Sally It's different.

Tom (*Groans*) No, no.

Sally Complacent. Men are complacent.

Tom Women are neurotic.

Sally Rubbish.

Tom Rubbish yourself.

Sally Rubbish with knobs on.

Tom With elephant's clogs on.

Sally Men!

Tom Women!
    (*Laughter growing*)
    I fancy a bacon sandwich.
    (*Sudden rising sound of trees rushing in the wind. And then the click of the gramophone and the Schubert song, first verse. The second verse comes in loudly, and then fades*)

Tom (*Close to us*) I know why! You turned it off when it came to the

bit about the crowing.
'And when the cocks crew
I woke.
It was cold and drear.
The ravens croaked on the roof.'
But it won't happen, will it? Nothing can happen. It's nothing.
Only the leaves. The end of summer.

Sally (*In sleep*) Rain ...

Tom (*Soothing*) Nothing ...
      (*The music fades*)

Tom There's that moon again. Hello, moon. 'Shine on, shine on, harvest moon, up ...' I bet you've had more people write tunes, more people write poems about you than any – well, except the sea. Yes, I think you lose by a short head there, dear. Still, you've got your finger in that pie as well, haven't you? You and the sea go hand in hand. Or something. But you haven't changed.

Sally (*Waking*) What is it?

Tom Hello.

Sally Oh.

Tom Do you remember the night afterwards, when it was all over, and I lay down there in the grass and that fox came through the garden with a white hen in its mouth? A killing under the moon.

Sally Still the moon!

Tom Because it isn't the same, is it? It's like a tooth with stoppings, like – I mean, think of all that junk up there, all that hardware, lying about, rotting. We'll be using it for a waste car dump eventually, you know.
I'm surprised nobody's thought of it already. Well — I have, I've thought of it, I ought to do something. I could make my fortune. That's how men make their fortunes, out of ideas like that. We could be rich.

Sally Do you want to?

Tom Oh, no, think of the problems involved. How'd you get them all up there, how would ...

Sally Be rich.

Tom Oh, that. Never thought about it really.

Sally Ha!

Tom We're all right.

Sally Are we?

Tom You turned the record off when the cocks crowed.

Sally It was only a dream. He was having a dream.

Tom (*Hums the Schubert*) 'Ich träumte von bunten Blumen, so wie sie wohl blumen . . .'

Sally I don't want to think about it. It reminds me of everything.

Tom 'Darling, they're playing our tune . . .'

Sally It's silly to get attached to a tune like that. We shouldn't have kept on and on with it. Playing it all the time.

Tom Go to sleep.

Sally I shan't play it again.

Tom (*Microphone voice*) 'Tranquility base. The eagle has landed.'

Sally Sleep . . .

(*Shifting of blankets. Silence. Then Tom's voice in the silence, very clear and alert*)

Tom The rain's begun again.

(*Rain on the roof, through the trees, into the river, falling more and more loudly*)

(*Sound of breakfast pots in the kitchen*)

Tom You know what your trouble is? You do know, don't you?

Sally Probably.

Tom You have an over-developed . . .

Sally Catch!

Tom What? Don't . . .

Sally Well, you're the one who pours salt all over your egg till it looks like a dandelion knee-deep in snow.

Tom Dandelions don't have knees. Anyway, you shouldn't throw things at me like that, first thing.

Sally Last thing?

Tom No, to get back . . .

Sally I shouldn't. (*Going out of the kitchen*)

Tom . . . over-developed sense of fate, of doom, of disaster. You don't feel happy unless you have that feeling on you. It's very neurotic.

Sally It is.

Tom And time-wasting. Life-wasting.

Sally Couldn't agree with you more. Pass the salt.

Tom All shall be well and all shall be well, and all manner of things . . .

Sally Where did you put the radio?

Tom I haven't seen the radio.

Sally You had it.

Tom Eustace sat on it?

Sally That was the record. (*Going out of the room*)

Tom What do we want the radio for anyway? Nobody's landed on the moon this morning. Have they? No. And there's nothing else we want to, need to, ought to, know about. At all.

Sally (*Returning. Fiddling with radio knobs*) It might be too late.

Tom For?

Sally Local news. It's before the main news.

Tom Local news? Here? What happens here? Nothing. Nothing happens here. Thank God.

(*Pips and then the announcer. Main news*)

Sally Damn.

Tom What is all this?

Sally I wanted to hear about the flood damage.

Tom How do you know there's been any?

Sally There was plenty yesterday. And it's rained all night again, hasn't it?

Tom Half the night.

Sally I hate it. The thought of it, the river creeping up and up towards us.

Tom It was raining when I first met you.

Sally It's like a monster, crawling, crawling across the ground.

Tom My hair was soaked.

Sally Like one of those monsters in the Science Museum ...

Tom Natural History Museum.

Sally Yes. Why did I just think of that?

Tom You weren't listening.

Sally Isn't it funny how you just think of things, they just pop into your head ...

Tom (*Patiently*) We met there, actually. In the Natural History Museum, South Kensington. It was raining outside at the time. Pouring with rain.

Sally I didn't think men remembered things like that.

Tom You've got a funny idea of men.

Sally Fancy you remembering.

Tom Fancy!

Sally I wish you hadn't.

Tom Charming.

Sally I don't want to think about them. Those monsters.

Tom Dinosaurs. Brontosauri ... Do you know, the last school I was at, but one, the one where the classics master played poker with the Upper Remove for valuable postage stamps stolen from their

22

fathers, that one – there was a craze for monsters. Waiting lists a mile long in the library for books about prehistoric monsters. I can't think why.

Sally I don't like to talk about them.

Tom But you're quite right, now I think about it. The river – like a monster – swelling and swelling, up and up, its slimy wet hands reaching out to get us, its inexorable tread over the marshy land, its . . .

    – (*Getting carried away*)

Sally (*Really angry*) Shut up!

Tom Sorry, I'm sure. Here – you're not really worried are you? We're quite safe.

Sally Are we?

Tom Look, if you are – I mean, I'll telephone someone, the engineers might build a dam. Or something. You're not really worried?

Sally It might be that.

Tom What?

Sally Or something else. Anything, anything.

    (*Tom lays down his knife and fork*)

    Don't you see, it doesn't matter what it is, the flood or the leaves falling and winter coming or – it will end, it's got to end. This summer. We've been too happy here.

Tom You can't be *too* happy.

Sally It doesn't last.

Tom Happiness does last, you know. Sometimes, often.

Sally No.

Tom Yes. A lot of people go on being quite content a lot of the time.

Sally Quite content!

Tom All right – happy, then. Yes. Happy. Downright, unashamedly happy.

Sally Not me.

Tom Now you're indulging.

Sally Now we are quarrelling.

Tom No.

Sally That's how it starts. It always starts like that.

Tom (*Mocking*) The beginning of the end.

    (*Silence*)

    I wonder if the hedgehog's come.

Sally (*Brightening deliberately*) Anyway – what will you do today?

Tom See if the hedgehog came.

Sally I put milk out.

Tom Do you know, people used to think that hedgehogs sucked milk from cow's teats, in the fields, at night?

Sally You said.

Tom And it isn't true, not at all.

Sally You told me.

Tom And they also said the hedgehog made love like human beings, belly to belly, one on top of the other.

Sally Because of the prickles.

Tom Spines. Only that's not true, they're just like other animals, man up on the back and the lady obligingly flattens her prickles and . . .

Sally How do hedgehogs make love?

(Both together) Very, very carefully!

Tom I might write a book about the hedgehog. Our hedgehog, I mean. How we tamed and befriended Henry Hedgehog and made him one of the family . . . Or a children's book.

Sally Someone's done it.

Tom I should have kept a diary about it. Damn. 'Dear diary, today man from planet earth first set foot upon the moon and our hedgehog ate a little custard, made with milk, five worms, one woodlouse and some cold leftover lamb, chopped very fine.'

Sally Your books!

Tom Or a country-life diary? Journal of a man of leisure and no means. How the fox trotted silently through the long grass of our garden, oblivious to the fact that meanwhile, back at Tranquility Base . . .

Sally Oh, shut up about the damned moon!

Tom I could ring the fire brigade for you if you like. They could rescue us on ladders.

Sally What?

Tom My God, don't say you'd forgotten it?

Sally The flood.

Tom Oh well – a man can hope.

Sally Do you feel a cold coming on?

Tom *(Sniffs experimentally)* Forgive me . . . should I?

Sally You lay in the grass.

Tom Ah!

Sally Wet grass. Out on the lawn.

Tom 'Out on the lawn I lie in bed,
        Venus conspicuous overhead . . .' Discuss.

Sally Auden.

Tom You're quite intelligent.

Sally Have you finished?

Tom Being cultural?

Sally Can I have your plate?

Tom Oh – what you should say is, have you had ample sufficiency? Yes, thank you. Sure? Quite sure, thank you. Please may I get down? (*Burps*) Oh – pardon. Granted, I'm sure.

Sally It'll be October.

Tom In the fullness of time, my dear Sarah, yes, I should say that it will. Given that it is now September.

Sally God!

Tom Have you anything in particular against October? Is . . .

Sally (*Shouting*) Shut up, shut up, shut up.
(*Silence*)
Stop being like that, I can't stand it when you're like that. Stop being flippant and silly and . . .

Tom And?

Sally I'm afraid.

Tom Yes.

Sally You know?

Tom Yes.

Sally Aren't you? Don't you feel anything?

Tom Feel what?

Sally That something will happen to us. Some terrible thing.

Tom The flood and we shall all be drowned. I'll build us an ark, the animals shall go in two by two, the hedgehog, the fox and – Eustace I suppose. We haven't got a kangaroo . . .
Sally, the flood is not going to reach us.

Sally Not that. Or it could be that. I don't know. Something. Don't you lie awake in the night and feel afraid that this will end in violence and sadness and death? It's like having bats, clinging to the inside of your skull. It's . . . that feeling.

Tom (*Gently*) No. I don't have that feeling.

Sally You've never had it?

Tom Oh, yes.

Sally But not now.

Tom Not now. Sally, listen – think of it. We'll stay here and it will be winter. Winter, and beautiful, egg-shell skies all glazed like china, and sharp frosts so that the grass creaks, and 'icicles hang by the

wall' and snow, very beautiful snow, coming softly in the night.
And fox tracks across the snow. And ice on the river and fires,
log fires. I'll chop down trees and make piles of logs like my
father used to, and I'll work in the morning while you make bean
soup and ... (*Sally snorts with laughter*)
(*Hurt*) Well ...

Sally Bean soup! What kind of a peasant do you think I am?

Tom A woodcutter's daughter. Well, all right, laugh – but it's just ...
I'm trying ... Sally, nothing will end. We have met and come
here and here we shall stay. I'll finish my book, and you will sit
at your machine and sew and stitch and make all those beautiful
little dolls and put small ads in the Sunday papers, so everyone
will buy them for Christmas and Eustace will purr by the fire and
the moon will be as thin as a new penny.

Sally I love you.

Tom But you see what I mean? Nothing will happen.
There. Say it.

Sally No!

Tom Say it. 'Nothing will happen.' Cross my heart and cut my throat,
hope to die if I tell a lie. Go on. 'Nothing will happen.'

Sally It's dangerous. It's tempting fate.
(*Tom groans*)
No.

Tom Do you know, the night that the city of Lyonnesse sank beneath
the sea, was the night of the new moon. Did you know that?

Sally Why did you say that? What did you remind me about the flood
for?

Tom Oh, hell.

Sally I want to try the radio again, there might be some news.

Tom I'll go out.
(*Wireless fading up*)

Announcer Here is a warning to motorists on the A 797 and surrounding
minor roads. The river Scheld has burst its banks at two points
near to the village of ...
(*Fade out*)
(*Door bangs*)

Tom Sally?

Sally They've evacuated Bankside cottages.

Tom I can't get down to the mail-box.

Sally Oh, God.

Tom It's pouring.

Sally (*Hysterical*) It's that moon, it's all your fault, it's that bloody moon.

Tom My fault . . .

Sally It sends people mad.

Tom We're not mad.

Sally And the tides. It affects the tides, doesn't it? And the crops and the rain and . . .

Tom And women in childbirth and cows in milk and the mating of the badger on moonlit nights and – Oh, for God's sake, you're primitive. I never knew a woman so elementally bloody primitive.

Sally Who started this? Who told it all to me? What the moon does, what it means. Who said, look, look, there's the moon, men on the moon, isn't it fantastic – God Almighty, I'd never have known about the damned moon, I'd never have thought about it.

Tom (*In a melodramatic voice*)
' The steersman's face by his lamp gleamed white,
From the sails the dew did drip.
Till climbed above the eastern bar
The hornèd moon with one bright star
Within the nether tip.
One after one by the star-dogged moon,
Too quick for groan or sigh,
Each turned his face with ghastly pang
And cursed me with his eye . . .'
(*Sally is crying quietly*)
(*Silence*)
Oh God. Sally, I'm sorry, I'm sorry. I didn't mean it. I don't mean any of it, I . . . Sally . . . love . . .

Sally I dreamt about it.

Tom What?

Sally I woke up and I was still dreaming, you know? And it was so cold, I was cold. I couldn't stop shivering. It was wet cold, I was drowning and I couldn't come up, I couldn't get awake. And there was that bloody moon.

Tom You frighten me, now.

Sally Something will happen.

Tom Something has happened.

Sally The winter will come.

27

Tom To you. It's happened to you. You're different. Perhaps we shouldn't have come here. We should have stayed in those long, cold corridors, among the brontosauri.

Sally Tom, I can't find Eustace.

Tom Useless Eustace. Cheer up, dry your eyes, and I will give you a nice surprise.

(*Sally blows her nose*)

And now we'll never know.

Sally What?

Tom Just think what there might have been for us today, in the post-box.

Sally Soup coupons.

Tom A long thin blue letter from America. 'Dear Mr Radlett, Each year we invite a distinguished scholar to our university to give a series of lectures to thousands of distinguished fellow scholars and riotously appreciative students. We will pay you 20,000 dollars per lecture, plus air fare, agreed expenses and in addition, provide you with a fully furnished house, equipped with deep freeze, well-stocked bar, daily cleaner, shoe-shine boy. In addition...

Sally Bills.

Tom And a further heavy advance on royalties from my publisher, so enormous has the demand been, prior to publication.

Sally Little buff envelopes from little buff men in little buff offices, demanding money.

Tom An order from the Soviet Union for half a million hand-made, hand-embroidered puppet dolls.

Sally He's been out all night.

Tom And now we shan't know.

Sally He never stays out in the rain. Cats hate rain. I called him and called him.

Tom Under the bed? In the loft? On top of the immersion heater?

Sally I looked and looked.

Tom 'Dear Mr Radlett, Her Majesty the Queen has asked me to...'

Sally Besides, he'd have come home when he was hungry, he's always at his hungriest in the morning.

Tom Let's have some coffee.

Sally I think I'll go out and look again.

Tom (*In the kitchen*) Come to think of it, I don't suppose you could turn out half a million puppet dolls, could you? Not on your own. And I'm no good, I never was any good with my hands. You'd

have to employ labour, start a cottage industry, you'd be the one
to make a fortune. Sugar ... sugar ... What are you doing?

Sally Putting on my wellingtons.

Tom He'll come back. They always do. Cats are a law to themselves.
Perhaps he's courting.

Sally Shan't be long.

Tom Oh look here, let me go, I'll go ...

(*Door bangs. Tom groans. Kettle whistles, higher and higher, then
behind it, the sound of pouring rain*)

(*Rain softer, Sally crying quietly*)

Tom Love ... oh, love ...

Sally I can't stop thinking about it. It's there, all the time, just behind
my eyes. It won't go away.

Tom Hell, I wish I'd gone, you should have let me go, I'd have found
him.

Sally When you touched him, his fur used to crackle, it was so electric,
he was so alive. Cats are more alive than any other animal. He
used to quiver all over when he was stalking a mouse out there
through the long grass. All those nerve ends. It wasn't him, was
it, it wasn't the same? Looking so awful, so ... so bloated and
heavy and cold and dead. Just dead. Nothing. He was so cold.

Tom He wouldn't have felt anything.

Sally Oh, how can you say that? How can you ever know? That's the
sort of fatuous thing people always say, callous, stupid people.
'They're not the same as us, you know, they can't talk so they
probably can't feel.' Do you know, when the stalks are cut off
flowers, they weep, they cry, do you know that? Scientists have
proved it, they've heard it. He looked so water-logged and dead.

Tom I suppose the branch just snapped and he catapulted down into
the water. Funny. I thought cats could swim.

Sally He didn't have a chance to swim. He might have hit his head on
a stone – anything.

Tom It was quick.

Sally How do you know?

Tom (*Sighs*) Look – look, if you think I'm not upset ... I liked him,
too. I liked that cat.

Sally He is dead.

Tom I'll buy us another.

Sally That bloody moon. That bloody water.

Tom It could have happened any time, it could have happened another way. He might have got run over.

Sally There aren't any cars here.

Tom No.

Sally I daren't go to sleep. I daren't lie down again.

Tom I'm here.

Sally You can't stop it happening, can you? You can't stop what I dream about, what I see.

Tom No.

Sally You don't know anything about me.

Tom No.

Sally I'm sorry.

Tom I truly was very fond of Eustace.

Sally It's raining. It's still raining.

Tom Look, tomorrow we'll pack things up – move things up here from downstairs and we'll go, we'll take a chance.

Sally How can we go?

Tom In a boat.

Sally We haven't got a boat.

Tom They'll send one for us. They're doing that, it was on the radio. They're rescuing people by boat. I'll telephone them in the morning.

Sally Will you? Will they really come?

Tom They might be on their way already. They've probably got us on their list. 'Evacuate tenants of Island cottage.'

Sally Oh.

Tom O.K? Better?

Sally I keep seeing him. His eyes were so huge and staring and bulging and dead. He was so dead.

(*Silence. Rain. Tom hums the Schubert tune*)

NO!

Tom Sorry. My God, though, the meaning you've hung around the neck of that song. One simple song about a dream of spring.

Sally And waking.

Tom Laden with your ponderous meanings.

Sally None of it was there. He dreamed it all. The ravens were croaking when he woke up.

Tom Go to sleep. Go to sleep.

(*Rain on the windows, softly. Sally breathing*)

(*Very quietly. The microphone voice*) 'Do you have us? This is Houston? Houston. Come in Mr President. Well, Buzz and Neil,

this has to be the most historic phone call ever made . . . blah-blah-blah . . .' and how impressed were you with all that?
Damned P.R.O. stunt. What did it feel like? 'Tranquility Base, the eagle has landed.'
(*Sings*) 'Here's to the next time . . .' Because you wait, my girl, they've only just begun, you wait till you're a popular holiday resort.

> (*Rain again, on roof, in trees, the river gurgling*)

The phones are dead.

> (*Pause*)

Sally?

Sally   Yes.

Tom   I said . . .

Sally   I heard you. I think I'll make a chocolate cake. Or would you rather have light fruit?

Tom   What's happened to you?

Sally   Light fruit?

Tom   Calm.

Sally   Yes.

Tom   We'll have to be a bit careful with food now, won't we?

Sally   There's plenty for a chocolate cake.

Tom   Don't you mind? Have you stopped caring? Don't tell me.

Sally   You ought to do some work. You haven't done any work for days.

Tom   Shall we have some cake for tea? Hot? Lovely sticky warm brown slabs of it, crumbling and steaming?

Sally   It's bad for you like that. It gives you indigestion.

Tom   And sit in front of the fire and have big mugs of tea as well.

Sally   The hedgehog didn't come this morning.

Tom   Didn't like the wet.

Sally   The day I met you your hair was wet and your face was wet and your clothes were wet. You looked most unattractive.

Tom   Damp among the dinosaurs.

Sally   I didn't fancy you at all.

Tom   What were you doing there, anyway? I've never found that out. What were you doing in the Natural History Museum?

Sally   You have to go somewhere.

Tom   Do you?

Sally   On your own in London, when it's wet.

Tom   How sad.

Sally I hate that place. I hate the way it smells.

Tom Musty animals stuffed with straw.

Sally Formaldehyde.

Tom Stagnation.

Sally But you have to go somewhere.

Tom Not now. You're not on your own in London now, you're here with me.

Sally In the wet.

Tom You are not alone.

Sally Aren't I?

Tom Maybe they'll just come for us – in the rowing boat.

Sally No. They won't do that.

Tom Why shouldn't they?

Sally If you wait and wait for something to happen, if you tighten yourself up and wait for it, and then it doesn't come, you ...

Tom What?

Sally I don't think they'll bring a boat, anyway.

Tom You know you enjoy it, you really do enjoy it. You're so damned fatalistic.

Sally You have to make it happen for yourself.
          (*Door slams*)

Sally (*Sleepy voice*) This is lazy.

Tom Bed in the afternoon.

Sally Lazy.

Tom When will the chocolate cake be done?

Sally Never.

Tom You made it.

Sally The electricity went off. Didn't I tell you?
          (*Sudden movement of bedclothes*)

Tom This is serious.

Sally Is it?

Tom Pull yourself together. What's the matter with you?

Sally You're so nervy.

Tom We've got to do something about that. No phone. No light ...

Sally Oh, but there's the moon ...

Tom No heat.

Sally Log fires.

Tom The wood's wet. It's too wet.

Sally Bed then. Warm in bed.

32

Tom Besides I haven't got an axe for chopping.

Sally Plenty of tins. No need to worry about food.

Tom Cold tins.

Sally You can get used to anything.

Tom No chocolate cake.

Sally You're so restless.

Tom If I go out and down to the river bank – well, as far as I can, and shout and shout . . . I could put up a white flag or . . . I'll think of something.

> (*Getting out of bed*)

Sally (*Lazy*) Come back . . .

Tom Got to do something. You're the one who started all this.

Sally No.

Tom Getting worked up. Socks? I can't find my socks. I'll have to learn not to tear my clothes off and throw them in all directions . . . socks . . . my dormitory monitor used to thump me for that . . . Radlett, you are a slut, Radlett, I just found your tie under the washbasin . . . Oh, here are my socks.

Sally You look ridiculous. What's the panic?

Tom You're mad.

Sally Nobody can do anything now.

Tom Or hysterical. Yes, that's it, hysterical. That's how it takes some people. Makes them go all calm and far away.

Sally Come back to bed.

Tom Sally, wake up . . . wake up.

Sally Now do you see? Now?

Tom I don't know what's hit you all of a sudden, I'm trying to make you wake up because O.K. something happened, I admit it, we might be marooned or . . . wake up, get up.

Sally Now who's changed. Yes, I did tell you, everything will happen now, it couldn't go on, nothing ever does. And you're shouting at me, aren't you? Angry with me? You never did that before. You're panicking now. Our relationship has changed.

Tom For God's sake.

Sally That bloody moon . . .

Tom Jesus, shut up about the moon . . .

> (*Sally laughs wildly. Tom opens the bedroom door*)

Sally Why move yet? I wish Eustace was here. He was warm. I wish . . . God, I hate this waiting . . .

> (*The door opens again*)

Tom I can't get beyond the terrace. The water's come right up.

Sally Come back to bed. Tom? Come here.

Tom Stop being bloody ridiculous.

Sally Maybe it won't rain any more now, maybe it'll go away, the water will creep and creep backwards, inch by inch, maybe the sun will shine.

Tom Well...

Sally We can't do anything. You can't.

Tom I wish I knew what you wanted.

Sally And don't you? Don't you know? Tom? Come here, come here, come back here...

> (*Rain again, and water rushing loudly. Eventually, sounds of deep, quiet breathing. Then movement of the bedclothes. The closing of a door. Rain. Then the Schubert song begins softly. We hear several lines of it, with the rain still*)

Tom (*Coming awake*) ... again ... I can't ... What? (*Pause*) It's dark. It's bloody raining again. Sally?

> (*Bedclothes. Footsteps across the room. Door opens. The music comes louder, up the stairs*)

Sally? I can't see a thing. Sally?

> (*The music comes to an end and the record scrapes on and on emptily. Tom goes down the stairs*)

Sally!

> (*A sudden great hammering on the front door*)

What?

> (*Hammering and shouts*)

O.K. O.K. I'm here, I'm coming. I can't see a damn thing. (*Bumps something*) Hell.

> (*Voices outside*)

I'm coming, I can't ... where's Sally, for goodness sake?

> (*Opens the door. Rain and running water*)

God, don't shine that torch in my eyes.

Man Are you all right?

Tom I don't know.

Man We've brought the boat. You'd best start to pack a few things, Mr ... I can't see this list properly ...

Tom Radlett.

Man Mr Radlett. And take anything you can up the stairs. There's a couple of us could help.

Tom I've got no clothes on.

34

Man Electricity gone, has it?

Tom Where's Sally?

Man Come on Dick, up here.

Tom I was in bed.

Man Bring that other lamp.

Tom Sally?

Man Can we come in then? It's all organised, there's no fuss, no need to panic.

Tom I bet you were a fire-fighter in the Blitz. All the signs.

Man Here, Dick. Everything's O.K. Seems to be. Now then . . .

Tom I've got no clothes on.

Man I'll watch where I shine the torch, sir!

Tom Look, there's someone else here, she's . . . Sally, I don't know where she is, I can't see a bloody thing.

Man Couple of lamps here, have to make do, I'm afraid. No moon tonight. You could start by putting some clothes on, Mr – Can't take all night over you, there's others to see to. Bad round here, it's been.

Tom (*Shouting all about the house*) Sally . . . Sally . . . Sally . . . Sally . . . Sally (*Runs upstairs shouting*)

Man (*Coming up the stairs*) Get your clothes on, now, pull yourself together.

Tom (*Quietly to himself, in the bedroom*) Sally – you made it happen, Sally. You couldn't wait for it to happen, Sally. You couldn't wait for it to happen. It's what you wanted . . .

Man (*Calling down*) Bring what you can up here, Dick.

Tom It wasn't anything to do with the moon.

(*Footsteps*)

Man Now then, get something on.

Tom What's that you've brought up? What have you got?

Man Gramophone. Quite heavy, that. You don't see many of them much nowadays. The old sort. See to get dressed, can you?

(*Sound of gramophone winding up. The Schubert song begins*)

Man Now look here.

Tom (*Quietly*) Oh, go away. Go on. Hop off.

Man Listen you –

Tom (*More angrily*) Get out. You heard me. Bugger off.

(*Music goes on. Footsteps returning downstairs*)

Man We've got a right one here. Playing a gramophone record, sitting on his bed with no clothes on . . . Told me to bugger off.

35

Manage that, can you?
(*Music louder upstairs*)
I'll see to him.
(*In the bedroom, Tom sings gently. The man returns*)

Man Now then, I don't bloody care what you want or don't want,
mate, we've come for you, you're on our list, we're not doing
this for the good of our health. We do it voluntary.

Tom Bloody fire-fighter. Can't you tell?

Man These the trousers? Got them?

Tom Sergeant-major, with it!

Man Shirt.

Tom Sir!

Man Pullover.

Tom Bugger off, I said.

Man Tie.

Tom I'll kill you. Get out. I'm violent, officer, sergeant, sir, I've done
it before, there's no stopping me . . . now get out. I'll count ten.
I said get out. One-two-three-four . . .

Man (*Calling down*) Dick . . . come here . . . I need your help.

Tom (*Making for him suddenly*) Get out . . . I'll kill you . . . I'll murder
you.
(*Thundering of feet down the stairs*)
Get out of here and into your boat and row for your bloody
lives, I'm not coming with you, not anywhere, I'm stopping
right where I am, sink or swim, float or drown . . . *out!*
(*Door slams. Silence. Tom breathes hard. Then very slowly goes
back up the stairs. Sound of the music starting again. Creak of the
bed. Over the music, which is soft, Tom's distorted voice*)

Tom 'Tranquility base . . . tranquility base. The eagle has landed.'
'Houston, Roger . . . Houston . . .'
(*The music gets louder*)
(*Outside. Rain and the river running high. Sound of a boat's oars*)

Man I'll have to put in a report. It's tippling down again now. Mind
that log, Dick. Let your right oar go. It's like the bloody war, as
well. All pull together. I'll put in a report. Watch it, Dick, watch
that . . . hold it, let her rest, let her rest . . . It isn't a log. Give
us the lamp, Dick. Hold it steady . . . pull her round a bit.
(*Pause. Torrential rain*)
It's a dead girl. Hold that lamp up, Dick, I can't see a bloody
thing. Hold it steady. A girl.

36

(*Rain and pouring water. The music has been faintly in the background. A little more loudly, until the water drowns it*)

Lizard in the Grass

Lizard in the Grass was first broadcast on BBC Radio 3, on 7 November 1971, with the following cast.

JANE	*Helen Worth*
JANE'S FATHER	*Denis Hawthorne*
CLARE	*Linette McMurrough*
MEGAN	*Jean Rogers*
SISTER SUPERIOR	*Fay Compton*
SISTER PATRICK	*Fabia Drake*
AUNT BERENICE	*Colette O'Neil*
WOMAN	*Doreen Andrew*
SISTER IMELDA	*Aimee Delamain*
JOHN	*Martin Jarvis*
GIRLS	*Elizabeth Proud*
	Olwen Griffiths
	Jane Knowles
	Jo Manning Wilson
SINGER	*Jonathan Cooke*
HARPIST	*John Marson*

The music was specially composed for this production by Geoffrey Burgon.

Produced by Guy Vaesen.

(Fade up the sound of the sea. Soft hiss and suck of wave on shingle. A soothing noise. Out of this comes the music. Played softly. Then a voice joins it)

Singer 'With lullay, lullay, like a child
Thou sleepst too long, thou art beguiled.'
(Repeats. Fades gradually. Sea again. Then Jane's voice, rather distanced)

Jane Is it the wind? I can hear it. I remember that. It moved the leaves about.
(Sea sound, a little louder. This noise could be wind, passing through elm trees)
I closed my eyes. I tipped my head back and then – then I opened my eyes. I could see the leaves. I could see the sky. Up and up. Up and up. *(Her voice sways a little)*

Jane's Father I pushed you.

Jane It was in a garden.

Father In the orchard. Every day. Almost every day. Never an end to it. You never got tired. Swing-swing.
(Above the sea sound, the faint creak of a swing)

Jane He pushed me, in the swing. Whenever I wanted. Up and up. I could see the leaves and then the sky. I heard the wind. I can remember that.

Father I was the tired one. You never tired. Every day, up and up, up and up.

Jane I remember the swing.
(Creaking. Sea noise a little louder)
Where are you?

Father Up and up . . .

Jane Don't go away.
(Father laughs)
Don't stop, don't stop. *(Jane hums gently)*
Swing-swing. I can see the sky through the trees.
(Pause, then urgently)
Are you there? Where are you? Don't go away. Don't go away.
(The sea fills, topples over onto the beach with a rush. Then a bell, clanging on and on. Jane's voice comes near to us, clear and in a panic)
Don't go away . . .
(She wakes. Sounds in the school dormitory. Girls talking, dressing quickly. Taps running. Bumps. Morning sounds)

Clare What's the matter with you?

41

Megan Jane Pace isn't up.

Clare What were you shouting about? You were shouting.
(*A bell*)

Megan (*Calling to the dormitory*) Second bell. Second bell.
(*Scurrying noises. Banging of drawers*)

Clare Are you ill or something? What's the matter with you?

Jane Oh . . .

Clare You were shouting and shouting.

Jane (*Getting up. Moving away. Sound of a tap*) I don't know. We'll be late.

Clare You'll be late.

Megan Jane Pace is always late.
(*Door bangs. Footsteps running. Jane rushing about to get ready. A small, anxious murmur*)
'Oh . . .' (*Door opens again*)

Megan Jane Pace . . .

Jane Yes, all right, I . . .

Megan Take an order mark.

Jane No, I . . .

Megan You heard. Order mark. Again.

Jane I'm coming. I'm ready. (*Sudden pause*) I dreamed about my father.

Megan You're not the only orphan in the school, Jane Pace, you're nothing special. Now you've got three order marks in a week. You'll be sent for.
(*Door slams. Silent dormitory*)

Jane (*Softly*) I hate you. (*More firmly*) I hate you. (*Pause. In a cold voice*) 'He who hateth his brother stands in danger of hell fire.'
(*Bell clanging, louder and louder. Then a different bell, lighter, a pinging sound, struck by hand. Silence. The school is at morning assembly*)

Sister Superior Jesus, Mary Joseph . . .

Whole school Bless us and keep us.

Sister S Saint Anthony . . .

School Pray for us.

Sister S Glory be to the Father and to the Son and to the Holy Ghost.

School As it was in the beginning, is now and ever shall be, world without end. Amen.
(*Silence. One bell ping. The sound of the whole school rising from its knees. Shuffling. The introduction to a hymn on the piano, faintly out of tune. It merges, as the singing begins, into the sounds*)

Jane is hearing inside her head. The creak of the swing. The sea and wind)

Father *(As though very tired)* Jane. Janey-Jane . . .

Jane I can see the sky. I can see the trees. *(Her voice sways with the swing)* Don't stop. Go on forever. Don't stop.

Father Jane . . . *(More tired)* Janey-Jane.

Jane Swing me, swing me.

> *(The swing merges with the singing of the hymn. The final piano chord, suddenly loud. Then sudden, total silence. One cough, hastily muffled)*

Sister S *(Clear, sharp voice)* Jane Pace will come to my room this evening, after prayers. *(Pause)* You may go.

> *(A single ping of the bell. The Schubert 'Marche Militaire' strikes up on the piano. Footsteps of girls filing out. Fade)*
>
> *(Fade up, Classroom. Desk lids banging. Murmurs)*

Clare *(Sharp whisper, very close)* Jane Pace . . .

Jane *(Startled)* What? What is it?

Clare What have you done?

> *(Other girls join in the taunting chorus)*
>
> Now what have you done?
>
> You've been sent for.
>
> You're to see Sister Superior.
>
> Jane Pace.
>
> You got an order mark.
>
> Three.
>
> In one week.
>
> You're for it.
>
> Again.
>
> What have you done? What have you done? Jane Pace, in disgrace, Jane Pace, in disgrace, Jane, Jane, Jane . . .
>
> *(A desk bangs suddenly. Scurrying. Silence. Scraping of chairs)*

Sister Patrick Good morning, Four A.

Class *(Sing-song unison)* Good morning, Sister Patrick.

> *(Pause. Then Sister imitates sarcastically)*

Sister P Good-*mor-ning-Sister-Pat*-rick.

> *(A murmur)*
>
> Listen to you. Listen! What do you sound like? Stand up straight. Stand up as girls should stand first thing each morning. Bright. Alert. Attentive. Jane Pace . . .

Jane I didn't . . .

43

Sister P You did not what?

    (*Silence*)

    So you are a mind-reader, Jane Pace? You know in advance what it is that I have to say to you, you are ready with your denial, ready with some excuse?

Jane No.

Sister P (*Impatiently*) Oh, that will do, that will do from you for today. Now, let us make a fresh start, let us begin our lesson all over again. Stand up, speak up, speak briskly – clearly and briskly. Good morning, Four A ...

Class (*Briskly imitating*) Good morning, Sister Patrick.

Sister P And did that not sound better? You may sit down. Quietly. (*Pause. Then speaks sharply*) Jane Pace!

Jane Sister ...

Sister P Are you asleep? Have you paid any attention to what I have been saying?

Jane No, sister. Yes, Sister ... I'm ... not asleep.

Sister P Your name has been read out this morning, in assembly.

Jane Yes, Sister.

Sister P You are a disgrace to this school.

    (*Pause*)

Jane Yes, Sister.

    (*Her voice repeats itself, becoming an echo. 'Yes, Sister: Yes, Sister. Yes, Sister' ... Into the sound of the sea. A rocking voice. The music again, gently. Then out of the sea and the soft music, a faint bell begins to toll. The tolling grows louder. In the end, only the tolling bell. When it fades, Aunt Berenice is speaking. She is finding it hard to say what she must*)

Aunt Berenice Jane ... Jane, dear ... I ...

Jane (*Excited*) Aunt Berenice, Aunt Berenice, I'm here, listen the pig farrowed, Bessie farrowed, there are eleven piglets, Stubbs is going to take me to see, I can see them, all of them, I'm going to see the piglets, I'm going to see the piglets (*Starts to chant*) I'm going to see the piglets, I'm going ...

Berenice Jane! Be quiet. Jane. Come here, dear, come here to me. Sit down, Jane. I want ... I have something to say. I have to talk to you, Jane, now, dear ...

    (*Pause*)

Jane I'm going to see the piglets. (*Suddenly realising*) What's the matter?

44

Berenice Now, Jane . . .

Jane (*Rising cold note of alarm*) What's the matter? Your eyes . . . I can see . . .

Berenice Sit down, Jane, sit down. This is very hard for me, very hard, you must try to understand, dear, you must think of me. This is . . .

Jane A terrible thing has happened. There it is. In the eyes of your face. A terrible thing. Is it Violet? Is Violet dead? What's happened to Violet?

Berenice (*Impatient*) Silly, child, do not be so silly, so frivolous! Oh, it is so hard for me, I can think of nothing to say, nothing . . .

Jane Violet . . .

Berenice (*Angrily*) Violet is nothing, you are not to chatter and prattle in this way. A cat is . . . is an animal, it is nothing, nothing.

Jane (*Coldly reciting*) 'Animals do not have immortal souls.'

Berenice Your father is dead.

Jane No. My mother is dead. I have no mother.

Berenice Listen! Oh, why will you not listen to me, you must listen, you must try to understand.

Jane My mother was dead before I was alive. My mother was always dead.

Berenice Listen to me. You are too wilful, you are a difficult child, you have been hard to manage, impossible to understand, and now you will not listen. I know nothing of children, why will you not make some effort, why will you not help me? (*Shouts*) Listen to me.

Jane (*Suddenly*) My father is dead?

Berenice (*Controlling herself*) Jane . . . there has been an accident . . . a terrible accident, on board the ship . . . it is . . . you are to . . . you do not need to hear, you will not understand . . .

Jane I saw it in the eyes of your face. Something, some terrible thing.

Berenice Robert is dead.

Jane But the swing . . . who will push me up on the swing? Who will push me?

Berenice Jane Pace! Jane . . . Do you still not understand? How selfish are you, child? Do you not hear me? Your father is dead, Jane. Your father is dead and you talk of games, of playing upon a swing. Your father is dead . . .

> (*Her voice fades into the creaking of the swing. Creaking. Then the whispers begin again, the girls' voices*)

Girls Jane Pace.

(*Separately*) What have you done?

> What have you done?
>
> What is it this time?
>
> Always you, always you.
>
> Have to see Sister.
>
> Jane Pace, in disgrace.
>
> Disgrace to this school.
>
> Saint Anthony pray
>
> Pray for Jane Pace
>
> Jane Pace.
>
> What have you done?
>
> What did you do?

> (*The whispers become urgent and then out of them, a single voice, sharp and close*)

Megan What did you do?

Jane I hate you.

Sister Patrick Jane Pace, stand up please. Recite what you have learned. What poem have you chosen, please?

> (*Pause*)

Well?

Jane A poem I found.

Sister P What is the title of the poem? What page are we to find?

Jane No, it isn't . . . no.

Sister P I beg your pardon? I am asking you what poem you have learned from the Blue Swallow Anthology of Verse. Or is it that you have been idle, once again? That you have learned nothing, know nothing?

Jane No. I found a poem. I have learned one. I do know one. Only not there. Not from there.

Sister P Jane, you are scarcely coherent, I can barely understand a word you are saying to me. Can the class hear what it is you are trying to say?

> (*Murmurs:* 'No. No, we can't. I can't hear.')

What poem have you to recite for us, Jane Pace?

Jane (*Clearly and loudly*)

'Audivi vocem,

Japhet, Ham and Shem.

Magnificat.
Shew me the right path
To the hills of Armony
Whereon the birds yet cry,
Of your father's boat
That was sometimes afloat.
And now they lie and rot.'
　　(*Total silence for some time*)
　　(*Fade in plainsong. The end of Compline. The amen. Then a single
　　bell, tolling. Fades a little. Jane knocks on a door. Pause*)

Sister Superior Come in, please.
　　(*The door opens*).
　　Jane Pace?

Jane Yes, Sister.

Sister S Close the door behind you, please. (*Sound*) Sit down.
　　(*Long pause. She is writing. Sound of the pen. Outside, faintly,
　　girls' voices calling, and the wash of the sea. Birds somewhere, in
　　cages. The silence becomes oppressive*)
　　Well . . . Have you anything to say to me, Jane Pace? Have you
　　anything to tell me.

Jane I . . . Sister?

Sister S I had thought so. I thought that you would have something to
　　say.
　　(*Silence*)
　　What does the word 'contrition' mean, Jane?

Jane It . . . Oh. I have to say 'I'm sorry, Sister.'

Sister S I see. Is that all?
　　(*Silence*)
　　(*Pause*) For what are you sorry?

Jane (*Mumbles at first*) I don't know, Sister. (*Suddenly loud and violent*)
　　I don't know.
　　(*Silence*)

Sister S (*Gets up. Movement across the room. She is speaking from the window*)
　　This is a very beautiful place. A beautiful building set in beautiful
　　grounds, beside the sea. Do you not agree with me?

Jane Yes, Sister.

Sister S Yes. Then are you unhappy here, Jane? Is your life at the Convent
　　of St Anthony so disagreeable that you must protest by these
　　acts of silliness? Have you some other ambition for yourself?
　　(*Silence*)

47

Sister S It is a long time since your parents died. You cannot remember them.

Jane I remember my father. He pushed me on a swing. He pushed me every day, when he came home. There was an orchard. I could see the sky through the trees.

Sister S Little things. Fragments of memory. Things you have been told.

Jane I remember. He talked to me.

Sister S Your Aunt Berenice has worked hard for you, Jane, she has done her best, life has not been easy. She took on a grave responsibility. How much have you thought of that? How much have you considered her? How have you tried to repay her?

(*Silence*)

You have a very great deal to be thankful for. God has no time for those who bear their crosses with such an air of self-pity. Your Aunt has brought you up, has done her best for you. Your Aunt is a good woman.

Jane Yes, Sister.

Sister S You are fourteen years old, Jane. You are not a small child now, not a baby.

Jane No.

Sister S And yet I have so many complaints, here, in front of me, so many bad reports about Jane Pace. You are not a stupid girl, Jane, not a fool. Do you think that you are stupid?

Jane No, Sister.

Sister S No. Only rebellious and wilful, only idle and time-wasting, only a girl who takes pity on herself and disobeys and makes life tiresome for others. And now, today, something else, some other piece of news about Jane Pace. A poem not learned. A lesson not attended to, the instructions of Sister Patrick not complied with. What do you think that you will make of your life, Jane, if you are to continue through it with that attitude?

Jane I *did* learn a poem. I stood up and recited it. I did learn one.

Sister S What poem did you learn?

Jane A...a poem.

Sister S Which Sister Patrick had given to you?

Jane A poem I found.

Sister S Found?

Jane I liked it. I learned it because I liked it.

Sister S You paid no attention to the lesson. You were asked to choose a poem, any poem at all, from the Blue Swallow Anthology of

48

Verse. And was that not good enough for you? Did you require a wider selection? Was there nothing to suit your peculiar tastes?

Jane I liked the one I learned. I liked it better than anything.

Sister S You set yourself up as a better judge than Sister Patrick?

Jane (*Angrily*) I liked it . . . I learned it because I liked it.

> (*Pause*)

Sister S Do you always do just as you like, Jane?

Jane No.

Sister S No what?

Jane No, Sister.

Sister S Did you go outside the school grounds alone?

> (*Silence*)

Have you been out of the school gates and down the cliff path onto the beach? Alone?

Jane Yes – Sister.

Sister S Knowing that such a thing was strictly forbidden?

Jane Yes, Sister.

Sister S Why? Why do you do these things, Jane? Why?

Jane I – I wanted to go for a walk.

Sister S You go for a walk every day, every girl in this school goes for a walk.

Jane I like going onto the beach by myself. I like to look at the sea.

Sister S You like it. Just as you liked some silly poem you had found for yourself. You do what you like.

Jane It is a beautiful poem.

Sister S Do you know what 'precocious' means, Jane?

Jane No, Sister.

Sister S Then you will go to the library and you will look up the word 'precocious' in the Oxford English Dictionary, and when you have understood its meaning, you will also understand that I do not like it. I do not like precocious girls. They are vain and they are prideful and they are silly, they think a great deal of themselves and their own cleverness, they care nothing for others. And you will go to Sister Patrick with the Blue Swallow Anthology of Verse, tomorrow morning. You will ask her to choose a poem and you will learn that poem by heart during recreation time for the rest of this week, and on Saturday morning you will come and recite that poem to me. And you will now go into the Chapel and pray to God to save you from the sins of wilfulness and pride, to give you strength to conquer your own nature,

Jane, your own silliness.
   (*Pause*)
Have you listened and understood?

Jane Yes, Sister.

Sister S You may go.
   (*Footsteps, then*)
Jane?

Jane Yes, Sister?

Sister S You are spending the week of half term here while your Aunt Berenice is abroad.

Jane Yes, Sister. I know.

Sister S I hope that it will be a happy time for you, Jane. I want you to be happy here. That is why I have taken so much trouble over you this evening, that is why I have been patient. But perhaps the week of the holiday will give you a chance to think quietly about yourself, Jane – about yourself and the chance you now have to make an improvement, to turn over a new leaf. Do you understand me? Do you think I may hold out some hope for you, after all?

Jane I . . . I don't know.
   (*Pause. Then Sister Superior sighs heavily, gives in*)

Sister S You will go now, please. To the chapel.
   (*The silence of the chapel. Then Jane's voice, very quietly*)

Jane Audivi vocem
Japhet, Ham and Shem.
Magnificat,
Shew me the right path
To the Hills of Armony
Whereon the birds yet cry
Of your father's boat.
That was sometime afloat.
And now they lie and rot.
   (*Towards the end, the hiss of the sea, growing louder. Above it, a sigh. Someone murmurs, in sleep. A mattress creaks, bedclothes shift. The dormitory. Outside the windows. The sea.*
   Clare is whispering to Jane across the space between their beds)

Clare Jane. (*Pause*) Jane.
   (*Slight movement, then silence*)
What are you doing? You're reading. I can see your torch. You're reading something. Someone will come. Somebody else

will wake up. You woke me up. Megan'll wake up, and then what? She'll call Sister, then. You'll have another order mark. You'll get sent for again. Nobody's ever had four in a week. Nobody ever. What have you got? What is it? Is it a forbidden book? You made a noise. You woke me up. You're not allowed, anyway. It's bad for your eyes as well. You'll go blind. People do. You'll pull your eye muscles and that'll be God's punishment. I could wake up Megan and tell her. What'll you give me, for not? Why don't you answer? What are you reading, Jane Pace? It's something bad, I know. I can tell it is. You're reading something terrible. What is it? What is it?

(*No answer. The sea, coming louder*)

(*Fade up a dinner table*)

Berenice She has no friends. No companions. She does not do normal things. She is not a normal child.

Woman And the reading.

Berenice That is what I do not like. To sit about so much, reading alone. Robert was greatly to blame.

Woman You have been so good, Berenice. I could not have done it, I could have done nothing, nothing at all. I am so bad in any crisis, I go to pieces, quite. Is that not true, Arthur? Arthur will tell you. That I am bad in a crisis. I could not have done such a thing. You have been so good about it.

Berenice But she is odd . . .

Woman Robert was . . .

Berenice Yes?

Woman Strange?

Berenice She is so . . .

Woman Difficult?

Berenice But then, I know nothing of children, nothing.

Woman There was always something about him. Robert. Something . . .

Berenice Oh, she will remember nothing, nothing of her father. Well – she will settle down at St Anthony's convent, she will . . . nuns have a way with them . . . I have always thought that . . . yes. She will adjust to circumstances, make friends, she will be straightened out.

Woman St Anthony's . . .

Berenice But Robert was always so polite. Perfectly polite . . . And the sea air. I am a great believer in the sea air. She will be in the right place, the right place, by the sea at St Anthony's.

(*Sound of the sea. Gulls. Now it is behind the dormitory windows. We are back there at night. Clare is still whispering*)

Clare What is it? Why do you have to read it at night then, under the bedclothes, are you ashamed of it? It is something bad. You will get into trouble again. What are you reading, Jane? What is it?

(*The sea sounds swell outside the windows. Jane's voice. She is reading*)

Jane 'The wind blowing very hard about North East, with a continuance for some days, occasioned great seas, doing much damage on the coast during that time, breaking down the banks and overflowing many marshes. The sad effects whereof were severely felt at Dunwich, when a great deal of its cliffs were washed away. With the last remains of St Nicholas Churchyard, and the Great Road, heretofore leading into the town from the quay.'

(*The sea sounds are growing more stormy. Voices floating on the wind, cries for help. Sudden slitherings of rock and cliff. Gale*)

'The sea raged with such fury that the Cock and Hen hills, which the preceding summer were upwards of forty feet high, had their heads levelled with their base.'

(*The storm lessens a little. Her voice is cleared, more solemn*)

'In the Chancel of St John the Baptist was a large grave-stone, which, when raised, held a stone coffin, containing the corpse of a man. Which fell to dust when disturbed. And the shore was strewn with the bones of the dead, the bones of women, the skulls of babies and young children. The long-buried dead, washed from their graves by the surge of the sea.'

(*The storm grows again. Cries again, through the wind. Then the tolling bell, growing gradually louder. Taking over. The storm is just a background. The voice of priest and monks, intoning the responses of the mass of the dead, faintly*)

Monks Requiem aeternam dona eis Domine

Et lux perpetua luceat eis.

Pie Jesu Domine, dona eis requiem.

Agnus Dei, qui tollis peccata mundi

Dona eis requiem.

Dona eis requiem sempiternam.

(*The bell tolls on, more and more faintly. The sea sounds, behind windows again*)

Clare (*Still whispering*) What is it? What is it? What are you reading? Why are you reading? Why aren't you asleep? Something will happen to you, Jane Pace. Something terrible will happen to you. What are you reading? You should be asleep.

(*Sea sounds fade*)

(*The dormitory. Daytime. Girls talking, banging about, getting ready to go away*)

Clare What are you doing?

Jane Nothing.

Clare I shall have to sit on my case.

Jane Yes.

Clare We're going home. (*Pause*) If I sit on it, will it break? The hinges might break. (*Pause*) I wonder what you'll do here. What will it be like, just with them?

Megan (*Calls out*) You're to leave Jane Pace alone, nobody is to talk to Jane Pace.

Clare (*Whispers*) Sister Imelda might let you go out and take the food to the birds. You can get round her. You might be O.K.

Jane I don't mind.

Clare They might give you cake for tea.

Jane It's all right.

Megan Clare Boothright, just you get on, you stop talking to Jane Pace, it's forbidden, it's not allowed.

Clare Well I can't shut my case.

(*A sudden screech of laughter goes up somewhere else*)

I can't take anything out. I need everything.

Jane (*Very quietly*)
'That when ye think all danger for to pass,
Ware of the lizard lieth lurking in the grass.'

Clare What?

Megan (*Calls*) It's twenty past. Just gone twenty past.

Clare Oh . . . Anyway Sister Imelda's all right, I've told you. About the birds. You're always going on about them. Just try asking her.

Jane (*Amused*) What are you worrying about me for? I don't mind. I don't mind anything.

Clare What will you do? It'll all be empty. Everywhere. Well – except for them . . .

Jane I don't care.

Clare You will.

Jane You'll be the last. Your case won't shut.

Clare (*Fiercely*) Look, I'm only trying to be nice to you, Jane Pace, I'm only risking getting into a row, that's all, you're not supposed to be spoken to, in case you didn't know.

Jane I wish you'd all be gone.

Clare Anyway, you've got to learn 'The Lady of Shalott.' All of it. That'll take you about a week, I should think.

Jane I know it.

Clare They'll make you go to Chapel all day and take long healthy walks.

Jane There are bones on the beach. Did you know?

Clare Shall I take my French book out? Then I might be able to shut it.

Jane How queer you all look, buzz-buzzing about. All in brown and yellow. Buzz-buzz-buzz. And only I am still.

Clare They won't let you go near the beach, anyway, you nearly got expelled for that before. You'll have to walk round and round and round the tennis court, with a book, all on your own. Like they do, when they're saying Office. Perhaps they'll make you go with them and say it as well. Perhaps they'll try and make you promise to be a nun. (*Giggles*)

Megan Half past nearly. Everybody's got to be ready when I say, and everybody's got to be ready together, we've got to be the first form down.

(*Movements. Groans*)

Clare Boss-pig.

Jane I shall go down the cliff path and onto the beach and walk, by the sea. I shall go into the ruins and look for the well.

Clare You'll get sent away forever.

Jane I can do anything. I can do what I want.

Clare They'll lock you up.

Jane I could walk a hundred miles along the beach and never come back. I could find things. There are bones on the beach.

Megan (*Calling*) Clare Boothright, hurry up, you're the very last and we've all got to be ready.

Clare Oh . . .

(*Two girls' voices begin to chant*)

Girls 'No more walking two by two
Like the monkeys in the zoo . . .'

Clare 'No more walking round the garden
Always begging Sister's pardon.'

All girls 'No more spiders in my tea,
       Making googly eyes at me.'
Clare I wish it wasn't only half term, I wish it wasn't only a week.
Megan It's time, we're going, we're going . . . Now!
Clare (*Hesitating*) Jane . . .
Jane (*Fiercely*) Go on. Go away.
Megan Clare . . .
Jane Go away.
       (*A loud bell. Everyone leaving the dormitory. Going downstairs. Fading. The Bell stops eventually. Silence*)
       I am me. I can do anything.
       (*The sound of the sea. Then the harp tune, playing gently. Long pause*)

       (*Fade up. The singing of birds in an outside cage. Faintly behind, the sea. Clank of a bucket handle*)
Sister Imelda (*Very old and gentle*) Gently – carefully. Carefully.
Jane They're flying up near the roof. They're afraid.
Sister I Only not quite used to you . . . pour the water gently, dear.
       (*Pouring into tin troughs*)
       Gently. Not used to your voice, do you see.
Jane Nobody else comes inside here, only you. Nobody else has ever been.
Sister I Well . . . I can't bend quite as I used to, dear. That's right, a steady hand . . . fill them all nicely . . . gently . . .
Jane Are you very old?
Sister I (*Amused*) Oh, yes. Yes.
Jane Have you always been here?
Sister I A long time.
Jane That one's coming down, look. He hopped down onto a lower bit of branch.
Sister I The singing finch. He's a bold one.
Jane Green singing finch.
Sister I And the waxbill.
Jane (*Reciting*) Orange waxbill. Red-eared waxbill. Golden-breasted waxbill. Blue-capped waxbill.
Sister I You remember . . . I like people to remember their names.
Jane They have beautiful names.
Sister I They know me. They're used to me. That's all it is.
Jane They're your birds.

55

Sister I Oh no, dear, no.

Jane That's what they're always called. Sister Imelda's birds. Everybody calls them that.

Sister I Come now. Don't stay too long, don't bother them. They don't like to be bothered, do you see.

Jane May I help again? Can I help tomorrow?

Sister I Oh yes, yes. Mind you carry the bucket back where you found it. Yes. You're a good girl.

Jane Were they already here when you came? The birds? All the birds?

Sister I Oh, no dear, no. They don't live too long, not birds of that kind. Only a year or two. They only came . . . I don't quite recall, dear, not just exactly . . . A little time ago. Now, we'll go this way, down the side path, by the greenhouses.

Jane But they have been here a long while.

Sister I Not those birds, dear, not the same ones. No. When I came here of course, we had no birds, no. Nothing of that kind. There was a Sister Cecilia who kept a few hens. Out beyond the orchard. Before the orchard was sold, of course. It's sold now. Yes. We had beautiful eggs then, beautiful eggs from the hens. On Sundays and Feast days we had eggs for breakfast. Oh, yes. But not these birds.

Jane Why did they come?

Sister I Someone gave them . . . someone . . . I don't recall. In memory, I think. Yes. Had someone died? I don't just recall, at the moment.

Jane When did you come here?

Sister I Just down here, that's right. Now, we rinse the bucket out, dear, always rinse the bucket from the tap. Yes. You're a good girl.

Jane There is a bird called a white-headed nun.

Sister I Ah. But not here.

Jane No. My father told me. My father went to tropical countries. He saw the places where they come from. They fly about in the trees. Just like sparrows and starlings do here. But coloured birds, such colours – scarlet and yellow and green . . . all flying about, anywhere. Think! Why are all our birds brown birds? Dull, brown birds. My father told me . . . told me about a lot of things. I can remember my father.

Sister I Wash your hands, dear, when you go in. Always wash your hands.

Jane How many years have you been here?

Sister I Ah. I forget, dear. I forget, just now. I had my jubilee, though. Were you here then? Had you come to the school? Oh yes, I had my jubilee day. Fifty years since I professed. I had a very wonderful day, dear. Oh, yes. Were you here? I don't recall.

Jane No. When you first came here, you were young. Very young.

Sister I Oh yes. Yes. Shut the door, dear. That's right.

Jane When nuns die, they are buried in the chapel garden.

Sister I Yes. That's where I shall be. Now put the key up on the hook there.

Jane 'It is generall
To be mortall.
I have well espied
No man may him hide
From death, hollow eyed.'

Sister I You've a head for things!

Jane Aren't you afraid?

Sister I Oh, St Francis called it Brother Death.

Jane I found a bone on the beach.

Sister I Yes. The tides. Ah, those poor souls drowned! And then the sands shift about, do you see, the currents bring this or that to light. Everything changes. I come from a sea-faring family. Yes. But it's a long time ago. Poor souls. Centuries ago. Old bones.

Jane My father was drowned.

Sister I Well, I shall be at rest in the Chapel garden, please God. I shall be at peace there. Oh yes.

Jane I picked up a bone and kept it.

Sister I No, dear. Don't do that. Things are best left. Natural things.

Jane It was lying on the beach when the tide went out. Just among the stones.

Sister I It happened here so often. So many of them, washed from their graves. Or never had a grave at all, poor souls, never at rest. That's how it is, always has been, just here. The sea took so many away.

Jane There was a town here. A whole city. Hundreds of churches. The storms washed it all away.

Sister I Long ago. Centuries ago, dear. Nobody remembers. Poor souls.

Jane How slowly you walk!

Sister I Old bones!

Jane Do you know, it was only the rich people who used to be buried inside the churches. The poor people went outside, further away from the altar. The rich people were buried out of the rain.

Sister I Oh, it makes no difference in the end. No. Now dear, wash your hands when you get inside, have I told you that? Don't forget to wash your hands.

Jane I can help you tomorrow?

Sister I You're a good girl.

Jane Sister . . .

Sister I I find the steps a bit steeper now, I can tell you! I used to run up these steps years ago, when I was a girl, when I first came to St Anthony's convent. Ran up, dashed all about the place. Sister Superior had to speak to me. Well, I smile about it now. But it isn't fitting, is it? Dashing about. And we thought more of such things then, little things. But they make no difference, you see, no difference in the end. I've all I want. But I do find these steps a little steeper.

Jane Goodbye, Sister.

Sister I Thank you, dear. They'll get accustomed to you, do you see, in a day or so. Move about gently, nice and gently. They'll get to know your voice, dear. Yes. You're a good girl.

Jane You are very old.

Sister I Now, I have just forgotten your name, dear. I don't for the moment recall your name . . .

Jane Jane.

Sister I Jane. Jane . . . Yes.

Jane Goodbye.

(*A door closes. Jane walks back to the bird cages. Sounds of fluttering, singing*)

Jane Plain Jane. Not like your names. You should be ashamed, with names like that. Don't they make you prideful? I should be prideful, if I were so beautiful. If I had your names. And all those colours. Look at you. Green as emerald. How vain you should be!

(*Suddenly, after a pause*)

How dull you are. Beautiful, coloured birds with your beautiful names. Twittering about. How dull.

(*Fade*)

(*Fade up. Rustle of nun's robes and footsteps along a corridor. Clatter of rosary beads*)

Sister Superior Sister Patrick . . . (*Nearer*) A word . . .

Sister Patrick Ah yes. Now, I have been looking in the lockers, the dormitory lockers, checking things. And they are a downright disgrace, a disgrace. Have you seen how things are left strewn about as though the school had been emptied after some alarm bell? How slovenly our girls have become? I have wanted to find you, I have a good deal to say about it. A plimsoll here, a shoe-bag there, broken combs, books thrown about anyhow, and everything with nametapes missing. Oh, I have a pile of unnamed garments, a pile of them. The school is becoming a junk-shop, Sister Superior, an old clothes emporium, everything is getting slack. And I am responsible for that side of things, I am the one who has that duty to carry out.

Sister S Yes, but just now, it is another matter, it is about Jane, Jane Pace . . . Have you a moment? Perhaps we could go into my room?

(*Fade. Fade up as the door closes and they are inside the room. Outside, a wind is getting up. The windows creak. Sea*)

Jane Pace, Sister. Is she happy? Is she unhappy? I have tried to speak to her, tried to make her feel a little more relaxed and at home. I should like to think we have made her holiday week a little . . .

Sister P And the poem? Has she applied herself? She has plenty to read, plenty of things to do.

Sister S It is a holiday . . . I thought . . .

Sister P But she has helped Sister Imelda, she has been allowed to potter about, the weather has been kind.

Sister S Jane Pace . . . I have her on my conscience. It is her eyes . . . something about her eyes. An orphan, of course, things are not easy.

Sister P She must make an effort. It cannot all come from others, from sympathy. The other girls cannot always be expected to make allowances.

Sister S She has been down onto the beach. She likes to walk about the beach.

Sister P Out of bounds? Is that altogether wise? Previously . . .

Sister S Oh, but it is a holiday, I have made myself plain that things are a little different just during the week of the holiday . . . Perhaps I have been . . . harsh . . . Perhaps it is not altogether a satisfactory life, holidays here, time with an aunt . . .

Sister P Not many women would have taken on that responsibility.

Sister S No. (*Pause*) She is . . . Her head is full of oddities, she has read too much of things she cannot take in, cannot fully understand.

Sister P Precocious –

Sister S Perhaps . . . it is lonely here for a child, the school deserted, other girls at home with their families. I am uncertain what to do for the best, how she can be taken out of herself, be entertained.

Sister P She is to read *Jane Eyre*. She has a panel to embroider. Poetry to learn. There should be no time for a head full of peculiar imaginings. 'This is the weather the cuckoo likes.'
That is what I have set her to learn.

Sister S Well . . . and there are the walks.

Sister P And she is a help to Sister Imelda. It is all perfectly ordinary, perfectly satisfactory.

Sister S I have only been . . . anxious. A little anxious.

Sister P As I am anxious now, Sister, anxious about the state of the school, the untidiness, the careless habits.

Sister S (*Half-listening. Looking out of the window*) The wind is getting up. We should bolt the windows firmly. (*Pause*) I am only thinking of the top dormitory. So empty for her. Empty rooms and corridors, Sister.

Sister P And thirty-eight members of the Community only one floor below?

Sister S Ah. (*Brisker*) Yes. Now, you were wanting to consult me about all this untidiness?
        (*Fade*)

(*Fade up. Dormitory. A tap runs. Is turned off. Outside, wind and sea louder. Footsteps come along the corridor outside briskly. Door opens*)

Sister P Well now, this will be something of a change, Jane, a nice, peaceful night and no disturbances, the whole dormitory to yourself! I see you have left a tap dripping. That is simply carelessness, is it not? Get out of bed, please, turn it off. Such things should never become habits. Tight taps and tidiness. Neatness. You would go through life leaving taps dripping, if I did not speak to you! Well, there will be none of the other girls to toss and turn and keep you awake, will there?

Jane It's empty.

Sister P Have you said your night prayers Jane?

Jane 'And if I die before I wake,
      I pray the Lord my soul to take.'

Sister P There is a little more to it than that, I hope. Are your prayers said as quickly and carelessly as your clothes have been put away? I hope not. Blouse sleeve inside out, skirt half off the hanger. Perhaps it all begins and ends with you, Jane Pace, all this untidiness at St Anthony's School?

Jane That's not fair!

Sister P Do not speak to me like that, please. Just because you are the only girl in the school and have been granted certain privileges. Our Lord is not fond of people who take advantage, of impertinent people. Now, you may read for a quarter of an hour, until you hear the community bell. You have been granted later bed-time, just for this holiday week, you should be grateful to Sister Superior for thinking of you in this way. She is making every effort to give you a happy time? Are you grateful?

Jane Yes, Sister.

Sister P What have you to read?

Jane 'By the margin willow-veiled
      Slide the heavy barges trailed (*Stops here*)
      By slow horses and unsailed,
      The shallop slippeth, silken sailed,
      Skimming down to Camelot.'

Sister P Now what nonsense have you made of that?

Jane I've learned it. I know it all. I know it by heart.

Sister P But have you no feeling for the meaning of words, the shaping of phrases, have you no idea of rhythm? What sense is there in a pause just where you have put a pause?
      'By the margin willow-veiled
      Slide the heavy barges trailed. (*Stops*)
      By slow horses and unsailed . . .'
      That is simply nonsense.

Jane They have found the site of Camelot. On a hill. A very high hill, with trees all about it, like a fortress. They found a man's skeleton, too, curled up in a trench. He died with his knees up to his chin, like a child in a womb.

Sister P Oh, how are we to manage you, Jane Pace? Why is your mind so full of immodest and morbid thoughts? What concern have you with skeletons and wombs. It is not healthy.

Jane But King Arthur lived at Lyonnesse, the city beneath the sea?

Did you know? It was like Dunwich. Everything went under the water. There was a whole great city, courts and castles and palaces, and the tide took it. People danced and jousted and argued. But they were all drowned.

Sister P I am wondering whether I should not fetch a thermometer. You wander so strangely, I am wondering whether you are sickening for some illness, Jane Pace?

Jane I have to read a book. I'm all right.

Sister P You have read *Jane Eyre*? That is the book set for holiday reading.

Jane Poor mad wife, locked in the attic.

Sister P And that is enough talk for tonight, however interesting the books may be, however pleased you are with your own cleverness! You have a head buzzing full of this and that, you will have bad dreams.

Jane Oh, I have good dreams! Do you dream, Sister Patrick?

Sister P I live a busy, healthy, active life, I have jobs and responsibilities, I thank God that I sleep a deep and refreshing sleep. I have no energy for dreaming.

Jane How sad!

Sister P Your last thought of the day should be thoughts of Our Lord, calm thoughts, gratitude to God and his Holy Mother for all the graces and blessings of the day.

Jane (*Quoting from the Catechism*)
'After your night prayers, what should you do?'
'After my night prayers, I should observe due modesty in going to bed, and occupy myself with thoughts of death.'

Sister P And so you have learned your catechism, Jane Pace! But this is not the time or place to recite it and show off your knowledge. I have not noticed such keenness in the classroom during catechism lessons!

Jane 'It is generall
To be mortall.
I have well espied
No man may him hide
From death, hollow-eyed.'

Sister P And do you understand the meaning of all you learn, Jane Pace?

Jane 'Man that is born of woman hath but a short time to live and is full of misery. He cometh up and is cut down like a flower.'

Sister P Morbid thoughts. That is not what is meant in the Catechism.

Jane 'I should occupy myself with thoughts of death.'

Sister P With thoughts of God and all His goodness, and the purity and safeguarding of your own soul, thoughts of a simple, godly life, a life that befits a young girl. That will suffice.

Jane Sister Imelda is very old. She talks about death. She is waiting for death.

Sister P You are not to be a trouble to Sister Imelda.

Jane I like her. I like to be with her. She comforts me.

Sister P And why have you particular need of comfort? You have been more fortunate than many children in your position, you should thank God for the sacrifices made by your Aunt Berenice, for the kindness of those here around you, for your health and strength and the gift of the Christian faith.

Jane Why should I not talk to Sister Imelda about death?

Sister P You are an argumentative child and it is time you were asleep. There is nothing left over now for reading, you have wasted too long in chatter.

Jane There will be a storm tonight. I can hear the sea and the windows are rattling.

Sister P The windows have been quite firmly shut and bolted, there is no need for you to fuss about the windows.

Jane Oh, I am not afraid!

Sister P Goodnight, Jane Pace, God bless you.

Jane Sister Imelda was born here, right by the sea.

(*A bell rings*)

Sister P (*Firmly*) That is enough chattering for one day. You shall have to learn a little more calmness, calmness and simplicity of manner, you should try and have a little less to say for yourself. Goodnight, now.

(*Door closes. Footsteps go away along the empty corridor. Windows rattle. Sounds of gale and sea. They fade. Silence. Then a gust of wind fades up. Windows rattle violently. Jane wakes with a cry*)

Jane Oh, the lizard . . . Oh . . . Oh, how empty it is. Nobody here. 'No tossing and turning, no disturbance.' No one . . . (*Pause*) 'That when ye think all danger for to pass,
Ware of the lizard lieth lurking in the grass.'

(*Through the sea sounds, the bell begins to toll, grows louder. Out of it, the monks' voices singing the Plainsong Requiem. Beneath it still, the wash of the sea*)

Monks singing Requiem aeternam dona eis Domine

et lux perpetua luceat eis.
Agnus Dei qui tollis peccata mundi
Dona eis Requiem.
Dona eis Requiem sempiternam.

> (*As the voices fade, the voice of John emerges. He speaks quite clearly in the room beside Jane, just as a man. No ghostliness. After his first few words, the other sounds fade, though we still hear the sea and wind at times, through the windows*)

John Jane. Jane. Jane.

Jane Oh . . . What is it?

John You were asleep.

Jane Not now. I lie awake for a long time. I always lie awake.

John Thinking.

Jane Remembering.

John How quiet the house is!

Jane The nuns go to bed early.

John And rise early. A well-ordered life! How good a life it seemed to me once! How easy! How much I wanted it, that quietness and simplicity and ease. No problems. And so no answers. No salvation.

Jane I know you.

John You know me.

Jane I ought to be . . .

John Afraid?

Jane But I am not afraid. I know you.

John Yes.

Jane I have known you for a long time.

John You know everything about me. And then you found a bone on the beach. You kept it.

Jane Here, in the locker, with your book. It . . . Sister Imelda knows.

John Sister Imelda.

Jane She is very old.

John Doesn't remember.

Jane (*Imitating*) 'I don't quite recall, dear . . .'
> (*They laugh quietly. They are at ease together*)
I love Sister Imelda. And she is very old.

John She will die.

Jane Soon?

John Very soon.

Jane They will bury her in the chapel garden.

John I had no grave, no burial. Do you hear the storm?

Jane When you lived here there was a great city, until the storms washed everything away . . . Everything fell into the sea. It flooded up and over the land, it was like a great mouth, sucking the city down, a great whale. The cliffs came slipping and crashing down, they fell into the sea.

John The Cock and Hen Hills . . .

Jane 'Which the preceding summer were upward of forty feet high, had their heads levelled with their bases.'

John That was a sight . . .

Jane Exciting.

John Terrible. It was all terrible. Night after night, with the sky red as blood and the water boiling, people crying for fear, children lost, cattle drowned, dread and danger and death.

Jane Like the end of the world.

John It was the end of our world. People ran out of their houses, women ran about in terror. The sea was like a great boil, rising and rising. And the sky. The terrible sky.

Jane What did you do?

John What I could. Little enough. And in the morning walked up and down the beach, searched the marshes, waded through water, gathering up the bones from tumbled graves, burying the dead.

Jane Sister Imelda said to leave the bone. Put it back on the beach among the stones. Leave it to the sea.

John I waded too deep into the marshes. Where there had been land, suddenly there was water, terrible, dark water.

Jane I should have taken back the bone.

John But you have it here. You kept it.

Jane And now I know you.

John You have always known me.

Jane I have your bone.

John You have me. You have found me.

Jane Can you hear the wind?

John I have heard the wind since I was born.

Jane And the sea.

John But you help Sister Imelda look after the birds. The birds with beautiful wings.

Jane My father told me about birds. I remember my father.

65

John Jane kept a sparrow.

Jane Philip Sparrow.

John My Jane. My Jane.

Jane There are sparrows here. On the garden. In the roof. Everywhere. Anyone may see a sparrow now. But your Jane kept Philip Sparrow in a cage.

John Oh, sometimes it came out and I could see her, through the window, just manage to see.

Jane Poor sparrow.

John It hopped about the room. It picked the threads out of her embroidery, fed from her finger, it sang. It made her happy.

Jane 'It had a velvet cap
And would sit upon my lap,
And seek after small wormés
And sometimes white-bread crummés.
And many times and oft
Between my brestés soft
It would lie and rest,
It was proper and prest.'

John You know me.

Jane Everything. Was she beautiful?

John Are you beautiful?

Jane Oh, no!

John I thought her beautiful. I thought her . . .

Jane You loved her.

John And then there was no hope for me.

Jane A priest may not love a woman.

John And so I was no longer a priest.

Jane Father Justin comes here each Saturday. He hears our confessions. He hears the confessions of the Sisters. What do they say? What wrong can they do? There is nothing to do here that is wrong, they have no sins to commit.

John And so no virtue to achieve?

Jane You were a priest.

John I heard her confession. But then the Bishop came, my desk was broken open with a chisel, my papers read, books opened, scattered about. There was a scandal in the city. I was dismissed my holy office.

Jane Where did you go?

John Nowhere. I was a boy in that town, my father had lived there, he was a well-respected man.

Jane You had sinned, loving a woman.

John A girl.

Jane But you had done nothing.

John Written things.

Jane Said nothing.

John Someone watched me and wrote a letter. And then the storm came, the greatest storm of all. I did what I could, what I had to do, comforted the homeless, buried the dead, picked up the bones. Wept over the ruined city.

Jane There were fifty-two churches here once. And turrets and towers and battlements and chapels.

John St Felix, St Martin, St Peter's-close-the-Sea, St Nicholas, St Leonard, St Michael, St Bartholomew, St Catherine and St Francis.

Jane There was the Priory of the Grey Friars and the Priory of the Black Friars, the God's House Hospital and the hospital of St James.

John Middlegate Street and Convent Garden, Sea Fields and Scots Lane, Duck Street and Leat Hill, Maison Dieu Lane and St Francis Meadow. My father had begun to prosper, he built ships. Dunwich was the home port for eleven ships of war. There were sixteen keels in the merchant fleet and twenty deep-water fishing vessels. He employed many men, he was a well-respected citizen. I was a priest. I was his only son.

Jane And now the wind whistles across the grasses on the cliff edge. Now nothing is left.
'Nettles grow on the cliffs
In clumps as high as a house.
The houses have gone away.'
Now nothing is left.

John There is a city beneath the sea.

Jane The bells ring. I have heard the bells.

John There are bells here. St Anthony's bells.

Jane Oh, these bells! These bells! I hate these bells. Waking up bell, getting up bell, dressing bell, assembly bell, lesson bell, lunch bell, recreation bell, study bell, compline bell, night bell, lights out bell. Ugly bells.

John But there are footsteps running along corridors, voices calling, people laughing, there is singing in the chapel, there are birds in the cages. There is life.

Jane I had rather have been here then. I should rather have been the other Jane. Your Jane.

John Who was a Lady and sat all day and sewed with a brown sparrow between her breasts for comfort and company, who waited to be given in marriage to an old husband, whose father could not love her because she was not born a boy?

Jane Whose sparrow was killed by Gib the cat. Philip Sparrow.

John I looked at her through windows. I watched her kneeling in the pews of the cold church. Her breath came to me, warm through the iron grille of the confessional chamber. I looked at her. I said nothing.

Jane You wrote to her.

John Letters I did not send, poems she would never see.

Jane But they found them and punished you and nothing has changed, nothing has changed, nobody is truthful or forgiving or just.

John There is Sister Imelda.

Jane Oh, Sister Imelda who does not remember this or that, does not 'quite recall', who forgets my name, forgets my face. Who is old, old. There is no one. My father is dead. I remember my father. That is all. I close my eyes and remember. He pushed me on a swing, he talked to me. He was always tired.

John 'Audivi vocem
Japhet, Ham and Shem,
Magnificat,
Shew me the right path
To the Hills of Armony
Whereon the birds yet cry
Of your father's boat
That was sometime afloat.'

Jane And now they lie and rot.

John You know me.

Jane There is no one. It is an empty place.

John You have me.

Jane There are other bones on the beach. The tide turns and turns them over. Nothing changes.

John Come with me.

Jane There was a great and beautiful city, full of life, there was work and play and laughter and the sound of feet in the streets, the trotting of the hooves of horses, the hammering for the making of tall ships, there was music and singing to the glory of God, and now there is nothing except the wind through the tall grasses, and bones upon the beach and bells ringing from beneath the sea. There were Robert Aleyn and Willielmus Rabbet and his wife Marjerie, Nicholas Codden and Jacob Gathercoal, Thomas Tucklove and Mr Christepennyfaker.

'Here Thomas Cooper, sometime bayly of this town
Incloséd is in clay.
Which is the resting place of flesh, until the latter day.
Of one sonne and daughters six the Lord him parent made.
Ere cruel death did work his spite or
Fickle life did fade.'
And Jane. Who married an old man and died of a child.
And Philip Sparrow, killed by Gib the cat. And now there is no one. There is nothing.

<dl>
<dt>John</dt>
<dd>Come with me.</dd>
<dt>Jane</dt>
<dd>'In vain do individuals hope for immortality or any patent from oblivion, in preservation below the moon. There is no antidote against the opium of time, which temperally considereth all things. Our fathers find their graves in our short memories and sadly tell us how we may be buried in our survivors.'</dd>
<dt>John</dt>
<dd>Come with me.</dd>
<dt>Jane</dt>
<dd>I have your bone. I have you.</dd>
<dt>John</dt>
<dd>Or else you should leave things. Natural things. Leave them to the tides. To nature.</dd>
<dt>Jane</dt>
<dd>I have no one.</dd>
<dt>John</dt>
<dd>I have no one.</dd>
<dt>Jane</dt>
<dd>I know you.</dd>
<dt>John</dt>
<dd>You have always known me. Come with me.</dd>
<dt>Jane</dt>
<dd>To the Hills of Armony
Whereon the birds yet cry . . .</dd>
<dt>John</dt>
<dd>Of your father's boat
That was sometime afloat.</dd>
<dt>Jane</dt>
<dd>There is the wind. Listen. The sea is like thunder. Like singing.</dd>
<dt>John</dt>
<dd>Come with me.</dd>
<dt>Jane</dt>
<dd>The windows are loosening in the gale.</dd>
<dt>John</dt>
<dd>It is generall
To be mortall.
I have well espied
No man may him hide</dd>
</dl>

From Death, hollow-eyed.

Jane I have no one.

John You are Jane. You are Jane.

(*The sea fades up more loudly*)

Jane I have always known you.

(*Their voices alter*)

John Stay with me.

Jane (*Sudden alarm*) But there are no birds, there is no sky. I have wanted to stay with them, the beautiful colours of the birds.

John Birds die.

Jane Killed by cats.

John 'Are not two sparrows sold for a farthing?'

Jane Phillip Sparrow.

John You are my Jane. Mine.

Jane My father pushed me up and up in the swing and I could see the trees and the sky through the trees. I could fly as high as the birds, the beautiful birds.

John 'In Lyonnesse the ladies lie.'

Jane 'In sea-cold Lyonnesse.'

John I have looked and never touched, sought and never found, asked and never had answer, knocked and waited in the silence. I have no one. I have been alone.

Jane I am alone.

John Listen to the sea.

(*The bell begins to toll, faintly, and then the harp and the single voice, as at the beginning, humming the tune, gently and compelling as a siren. The voices begin to fade further into the sounds*)

Jane Oh, I can hear . . .

John The voices . . .

Jane And the bells.

John The music.

Jane Oh, the bells, I can hear the bells . . . the bells . . .

(*The sea gradually drowns their voices. Fade up the monks singing*)

'Requiem aeternam,

Dona nobis requiem sempiternam.

Amen.'

(*After the Amen fades, the sound of the sea, and a single, tolling bell. In the end there is only the bell, tolling*)

The Cold Country

The Cold Country was first broadcast on BBC Radio 3, on 3 October 1972 with the following cast.

CHIP	*Terry Scully*
OSSIE	*Jon Rollason*
JO	*Ian Richardson*
BARNEY	*Sean Barrett*
YOUNG BARNEY	*Jane Knowles*
BARNEY'S MOTHER	*Kate Binchy*
YOUNG JO	*Jane Knowles*
JO'S SISTER	*Helen Worth*
WOMAN	*Kate Binchy*
SINGER	*Kevin Smith*
MOUTH ORGANIST	*Alfie Kahn*

The music was specially composed for this production by Geoffrey Burgon.

Produced by Guy Vaesen.

The Cold Country
> (*Sound of the Antarctic wind whistling. Out of this comes a counter-tenor singing Geoffrey Burgon's setting of the 'Lyke-Wake Dirge'*)
This ean night, this ean night,
Every night and all,
Fire and fleet and candle-light,
And Christ receive thy soul.

When thou from hence doest pass away,
Every night and all,
To Whinny-Moor thou comest at last,
And Christ receive thy soul.

If ever thou gave either hosen or shoon,
Every night and all,
Sit thee down and put them on,
And Christ receive thy soul.

But if hosen and shoon thou never gave nean,
Every night and all,
The Whinnes shall prick thee to the bare beane,
And Christ receive thy soul.

> (*As the song fades, the sound of the wind is heard from inside the tent. Ossie is playing 'Roses of Picardy' on the mouth-organ. Chip and Barney are playing 'Snap'. The cards are laid down, faster and faster*)

Chip	Snap!
Barney	Blast you!

> (*They play on for a moment*)

Chip	Snap!
Barney	You've got the whole bloody pile, look at them!
Chip	I know,
Barney	What is it about me?
Chip	Your reflexes, you're not quick enough on your reflexes. Practice, that's all you need, plenty of practice. It'll come with time and that's what we've got here, isn't it? I mean, you develop an eye, you know? And you learn to speak at the same second you've seen the cards. SNAP! See? It's only a question of co-ordination. (*Barney grunts*) Ready are we? Off we go.

73

(*Sound of cards again*)

Jo (*From beside the radio. Excited*) Here ... here listen. Shut up a
   minute, Ossie (*Mouth-organ ceases*) I thought I heard something
   then. (*Pause. The card playing goes on*)
   I did, I'm positive I did. I heard something ... a crackle. I got a
   connection.

Barney Snap!

Chip Nope. Yours is the donkey, mine's the horse. You always get
   caught out on those two. You've not got to be *too* quick, that's
   the whole art. Quick, but not too quick.

Jo Will you two shut up and listen?

Chip What to?

Jo I've told you, the radio was working. I had a connection then,
   I definitely heard something.

Chip Well I didn't.

Barney No.

Jo Well how could you? Snap-snap-snap, that's all you ever do. And
   Ossie, playing that bloody thing. Of course you couldn't hear,
   none of you. But *I* heard.

Ossie (*Patiently*) Jo ... well, maybe you did, all right, but you can't
   get it again, can you?

Jo It was *something*.

Ossie We've been here three weeks and every day you've thought you
   heard something. *Thought* you did. But you didn't, it's a
   delusion, Jo, it's like the mirage of an oasis in the desert, because
   that's the stage we've reached. You didn't hear anything.
   Nobody did, nobody can. (*Raised voice*) The radio's dead, Jo, it
   isn't working. IT'S DEAD.

   (*Silence in the tent*)

Barney Yes, well ...

Chip Want another game?

Barney No, I've had enough.

Ossie I'll tell you something. In all the books I've ever read about
   explorers and expeditions, all the accounts of parties in the Arctic
   and the Antarctic, and crossing the oceans on a raft and climbing
   Everest and riding camels over the desert ... all of them, do you
   know what they say? They always tell you how bloody marvell-
   lous all their mates were, how patient and reliable and keeping
   their peckers up and life and soul of the party ... nobody ever has
   a cross word, nobody ever gets on anybody else's nerves,

74

they're all such great blokes, they're all so long-suffering . . . well, I'll tell you what. *It isn't true.* I've found that out. So have you, if you dare to admit it. And when I get home . . . because I will, don't let's be downhearted, isn't that what Jo's always saying? When I get home, I'll write a book like they've never read before, I'll tell them how it really is. We've been marooned in a tent in a blizzard for three weeks and we're driving one another bloody mad. We can't stand one another can we? Well maybe there's something wrong with us, maybe we're not 'Great guys'. Not the stuff heroes are made of. Jo wants to be a hero, don't you, Jo? That's why he came here. He won't admit it but it's true. He wants medals and a blue plaque on his house after he's dead. But maybe we're not like that. I don't know.

Barney I don't know either. But we've been all right tonight haven't we? Quite nice and amiable, I thought . . . having a game of cards, you playing your mouth organ . . . all very cosy. All right, let's enjoy it while we can. God knows, we haven't much else left to enjoy.

Jo We mustn't start getting depressed. That sort of thing spreads like a disease.

Chip They told you that in all the lectures, didn't they Jo? Like they told us in the army. Troop morale, they call it.

Jo We're not troops.

Chip Aren't we? Pardon me for breathing, I thought you were the C.O. You remind me of a C.O., do you know that?

Jo I think I'll ignore that.

Chip British of you.

Ossie And why the hell don't you call it a day with that radio, Jo, I can't stand watching you fiddling with it from morning till night. Let's face it, you're not going to make it work, are you? Why not just leave it?

Jo That's typical of the lot of you, that's typical of your whole attitude, isn't it? 'Just leave it. Let it ride. Why bother. What's the use? Give in, why don't we?' What sort of men are you, for God's sake? If that's your attitude, why don't we all go outside and lie down face first in the snow and die? Why are we bothering at all? Have you asked yourselves that?

Chip Oh, we're here, because we're here, because we're here, didn't you know that? And how do you think we'd have got on in *that* little lot in the war?

Jo The same as most of them did. We'd have faced up to it.

Barney God Almighty, do you really believe that?

Jo Do you know, I don't really understand you any more. You're not the blokes I came out here with.

Chip Maybe he's right, Barney. We're not so different from the men in the trenches are we? Well, are we? They coped. Never say die, like I told you.

Ossie They died.

Barney So shall we.

Jo No. We are not going to acknowledge that risk. If we start believing in it, we *have* given in. And we are not going to give in.

Chip That's right, troops, keep up the old morale.

Jo It's Ossie. Making all sorts of snap judgements. We don't get on, he says, we're driving one another mad. Well I think we're doing all right. As well as anyone else would do under the circumstances. I think . . .

Barney Oh, spare us the sermon.

Ossie O.K., O.K., forget it, I only said . . .

Chip (*Interrupting quickly*) I say, I say, I say, my aunt's gone to the West Indies.

Ossie Jamaica?

Chip No, she went of her own accord. (*Pause*) Well come on! . . . All right, try again. I say, I say, I say, my Aunt's gone to the *East* Indies.

Ossie Jakarta?

Chip No, she went by plane.

Jo Oh, for God's sake!

Chip Barney, why do cows wear cow-bells?

Barney I don't know, Chip, why do cows wear cow-bells?

Chip Because their horns won't work. Da-da-dee-da-da-DA!

    (*Silence*)

    Oh, I give up, I do really.

Jo Good.

Chip What's on your mind anyway, Jo?

Jo Oh, nothing, nothing. How to make you lot get off your backsides. Whether we're going to let ourselves live or die. Because it's up to us, you know. What we're doing here, what it's all about. What went wrong.

Ossie Nothing went wrong, it was an accident. Entirely unpredictable. Like all these things.

Jo No, not an accident. A miscalculation. We should have taken proper notice of the weather signs. We should have stayed at the last camp, instead of being bloody stupid and pressing on.

Barney Well we didn't, so that's that and all about it. You stop trying to make yourself into a martyr, just because you were the one who chose to go on and try and get into contact with the others again, instead of waiting. Look, we don't blame you.

Jo Thank you.

Barney Unless you want us to. Is that it? So you can go into an orgy of contrition and self-abasement?

Chip Leave it alone, Barney.

Jo All you can bloody do is sit there and play SNAP and crack jokes, and Barney tells stories and . . . look, we're not here for *fun*. All right, I made an error and we're here for the moment. But we're not letting it go at that are we? *I'm* not. We've got to do something. We owe it to ourselves to do something, because that's the kind of men we are. We don't give in. And we've got to try and find the others. We have *got to do something*.

Barney You say that every day, did you know? Or even twice a day.

Chip Why don't you fancy staying here, Jo? Are you afraid of dying?

Jo No. I don't think so. I am prepared to face the possibility, though I'm not prepared to give in to it. But I've been in dangerous situations enough times before.

Barney Bully for you.

Chip He wasn't a pack leader in the Cubs for nothing you know.

Barney You've got it all nicely sewn up, haven't you, Jo?

Jo It's a question of coming to terms with things as they are.

Chip What did the boy worm say to the girl worm?

Ossie I don't know, what?

Chip 'Let's make love in dead Ernest.'

Jo (*Thumping the table*) We've got to do something!

Ossie Do what, that's all I'd like to know. Do what?

Chip Have a toffee. You know, that's just the kind of thing that would happen. Stranded in the Antarctic with a strictly limited supply of basic food rations and an inexhaustible supply of toffees. That appeals to me. It appeals to my sense of the incongruous.

(*Ossie begins to play 'Roses of Picardy' again. Barney hums*)

Barney I had one of those only the bell fell off.

Jo The wireless is not working. We've got to face that.

Chip My dear chap, we faced it days ago. Weeks ago! You're the one
    who's been struggling on.

Jo I'm an engineer. I'm a practical man. I believe in sticking at it.
    Doing something.

Chip Suit yourself. How do you make a Venetian blind?

Jo (*Absently, as though it were a sensible question*) Poke his eyes out.
    Now look, one of us is going to have to leave here, on foot, on
    their own, and try and find out exactly where we are . . . how far
    from the ridge, how far from the Sound, and what would be the
    best way of trying to get back, or else, go on and hope to find the
    others. Or put out another flare. Something. This blizzard can't
    go on indefinitely.

Chip So you've said for the last three weeks. I don't believe it's going
    to stop for months. Months and months. I doubt if it will ever
    stop, personally. I think the whole world's coming to an end.

Jo (*Ignoring him*) We agreed on a reconnaissance. Didn't we?
    Ossie, will you please stop playing that bloody mouth-organ?
    (*Abrupt silence*)
    Thank you. Now, the real question is, who goes?

Chip Listen.

Jo What?

Chip *Listen.*

Jo I can't hear anything.

Chip Precisely. The wind's died down, hasn't it?
    (*They listen. Silence*)

Barney By God, it has too! It's gone quiet. It's bloody marvellous.

Jo I'm going outside to have a look.

Chip That's a good idea. I'll come with you.

Jo You stay where you are.

Barney Watch what you're doing out there Jo.

Jo What do you think I am?

Chip (*Mutters*) Bloody Camp Commandant . . . sir!

Jo What?

Chip I said, I call my dog Isiah.

Jo What?

Chip No, you don't say 'What?' you say 'Why?' Well, go on then,
    say it . . . 'Why?'
    (*Silence. Jo has gone out of the tent. A brief howl of wind as the*
    flap opens and closes)

Barney O.K. Keep your hair on, I'll say it. 'Why?'

  Chip No, I wanted him to say it. He'll never bloody co-operate.

Barney I'll put the cards away.

  Chip Ossie's right, you know, aren't you Ossie? About the way we get on one another's nerves the whole time. I was brought up a Christian, Barney, I was taught to love my neighbour. It counts, they said, every day, in every way, it counts. And look at us. You're my neighbour, he's my neighbour . . . I'm *his* neighbour. Christ!

Barney We're not exactly living under normal conditions, are we?

  Chip Is that relevant?

Barney I'm damn sure it is. Well, aren't you? Think about it.

  Chip No, I don't think it counts, does it? What *we* think. Not in the last resort. And this *is* the last resort.

  (*Ossie starts to play his guitar and sing*)

 Ossie 'And then we came to that cold country
  Where the ice and snow do lie,
  Where there's ice and snow,
  And the great whales blow,
  And the long night does not die.'

Barney I went camping in the woods with my brother once. About six or seven, I was . . . he was ten. We went, oh, five or six miles, right up beyond the farm and into the woods there. It's fantastic in spring, you know, the whole ground is just blue, as far as you can see, that marvellous sort of hazy blue. And there are wood anemones as well as the bluebells. Well, or there were. They felled it, felled the whole lot, put up a conifer plantation. Quick profit, you see, in conifers, they're all doing it. But that was later, before the old man died. This time I'm talking about, it was still real woodland. We took a tent and blankets and chocolate and stuff . . . we went right in as far as we dared, off the paths and down to where there was a stream. We stayed there all night. I was scared to death. I remember that. And when I was scared I blamed my brother for taking me there, for being with me there. If we'd have died . . . and I was sure we were going to, I was so scared, I'd have died blaming him. I think he was scared as well, only he didn't say much. The jays kept screeching. Jays and owls. Owls are the augurs of death. And in the wood at night, nothing's ever still. There are cracks and creaks and the wind sifting through the leaves. It came over all cloudy, and there was no moonlight. No light at all. We just lay there in the wood in the darkness. I hardly dared to breathe. But it was fantastic, now I think back. I'll never forget it. I felt as if there was nobody but us left in the world. I felt we'd never get back. I'd forgotten that feeling . . . till now. And at the beginning, I was blaming Jo, wasn't I? Because he made the wrong decision. The same as I blamed my brother. You don't change, inside you, I mean. Not really.

Chip Have a toffee?

Barney You're the same person you always were.

Chip I'm going outside to see what's happened to him.

> (*Fade*)
>
> (*Fade up. Ossie playing the guitar and singing*)
> 'Today you may be alive, dear man,
> With many a thousand pound.
> Tomorrow you may be dead, dear man,
> And your body be laid under ground.
> With one turf at your head, O man,
> And another at your feet.
> Thy good deeds, and thy bad, O man,
> Will all together meet.'

Ossie Hey, I wonder which this is.

Jo What?

Ossie A good deed or a bad. Coming here.

Jo Good, naturally. All exploration is good. Any trial of strength, any contest with the natural elements, any attempt to prove yourself is bound to be good. There's no question.

Barney Bad. It's pointless, it's foolhardy. I've just realised that, this last few days. Look where it got us.

Jo That doesn't mean the whole thing has been bad . . . just because it's gone wrong. Or that it would have been good if it had worked out.

Chip It's natural then, isn't it?

Ossie I don't know. I don't know at all, it's too complicated.

Chip Look at us . . . we can't even agree over a little thing like morals!

Jo Morals don't come into it. Practical issues do.

Chip That's my boy! Do something . . . anything. Act first, think later, for action is a virtue. (*Pause*) 'Waiter, this coffee tastes like earth.' (*Pause. He waits. Coughs*) I said . . .

Barney Oh . . . yes, sir, sorry. 'Yes, I'm not surprised, sir, it was *ground* this morning.'

> (*Jo snorts with a laugh*)

Chip Here, he laughed . . . he actually bloody laughed! Can I have that in writing, Jo?
(*Fade*)
(*Sound of a pan being scraped out*)

Jo Supper!

Chip Cheers!
(*They collect their plates. Start eating*)

Barney How many square meals have we left, anyway?

Jo We're all right for a bit. I'm keeping my eye on it.

Chip I suppose you think you're in charge, and in your judgement, it's better for our morale if we don't know the worst. You're like a bloody doctor. 'Am I dying, doctor?' 'There, there, have a nice drink of water.'

Barney There's always plenty of toffee.

Chip This meat tastes a bit off . . . sort of, powdery.

Barney It always tastes like that.

Chip Never.

Ossie It does, you know.

Chip Never, I swear it's different. (*Pause*) Well, the lot I've got is different. Oh, what the hell. I suppose I'd rather eat than be eaten, which is what'll be happening, soon enough.

Ossie No it won't, there aren't any worms out here.

Barney Do you mind? Listen, it was fantastic outside, it was marvellous . . . it reminded me of Hans Andersen. Did you ever read that when you were a kid? You should have come with us, Chip.

Chip Too bloody cold.

Barney It was worth it. I'd have stayed out there as long as you like. I didn't care how cold it was. The wind had died down and there was all that moonlight. Beautiful. There was a queer sort of bluey sheen over everything. It glimmered. And not a sign of life. Nothing. Not a bird or an animal, not a tree, not a plant. Scentless and silent . . . and us, standing there. It sounds like a sort of limbo, doesn't it? But I could have walked off and I could have gone on and on, I'd never have wanted to come back.

Chip You'll have me in tears, Barney, you've such a lovely turn of phrase.

Barney It was like a paradise, I'm telling you.

Ossie It's no Paradise, Barney, you're deluded. It's much like the rest of the world and the world is a bleak place. You look for a bolt hole, that's all, for something you can pull over your head to muffle the terrible noises.

Barney You've got a jaundiced viewpoint because you haven't got any family . . . there's only you. It makes a difference.

Chip What about you, Jo?

Jo Me? I'm a scientist. I'm a practical man.

Ossie That doesn't mean you've no feelings.

Jo Who said that it did?

Barney What we're all trying to say is that there is some underlying reason why each of us chose to come here. Below the apparent reason, that is. Something unconscious and to do entirely with your own particular personality. And we all came for different reasons.

Jo You may have.

Chip You've got your reason . . . and I know what it is.

Jo Well of course you do. It's a challenge. A question of discovery . . . of doing the job you know you can do, under the most impossible conditions. You're stretching yourself, to see just how far you can go.

Chip Oh, there's more to it than that, you'd be amazed. Have a toffee.

Jo I'm sick to death of toffees.

Barney If you pull out a filling, it's a long way to the dentist.

Chip Good . . . I can't stand them.

Jo He's right. We can't afford to be careless, to run the risk of any unnecessary injuries.

Chip Oh, for God's sake, you're too bloody pompous to live!

Barney Hadn't we better talk about this search party?

Chip Tactful!

Jo Tomorrow, weather permitting, one of us sets off on a reconnaissance. That's agreed?

Chip Yes.

Barney I volunteer.

Jo Nobody volunteers. We pick straws.

Ossie Oughtn't you to stay out of it, Jo? To begin with, you're senior and you're the only one who knows much about the wireless.

Chip The wireless is dead. We've given that up completely.

Jo Yes. And I'm not essential at this stage. No one of us is, so we all pick.

Barney How far are we planning to go?

Jo Either due North or due South, whichever looks the most promising, and always taking all precautions and never going beyond a point at which we are certain of being able to return without involving those left behind in a rescue operation.

Chip That doesn't account for accidents.

Barney Crevasses.

Jo In case of accident, send up a flare. There are three left.

Chip I still think two of us ought to go out, and two stay behind.

Jo We cannot risk two lives at this stage.

Chip I fail to see why. We're likely to die soon anyway.

Jo I'll ignore that.

Barney How do we pick?

Jo Screws of paper out of a tin lid. I've marked one with an X. The rest are blank.

Barney Listen.

Chip What?

Barney Can't you hear it?

(*Faintly, the wind has been getting up. Now there is a thin howl, and the soft pattering of snow on the tent*)

Chip Nothing much. A bit of snow.

Jo I'll have a look.

Ossie It always starts quietly.

Jo If the blizzard really gets up again, we'll have to wait.

Barney It's been three weeks. What if it's another three? How long *can* we wait?

Jo We don't look ahead. We work from day to day. We plan just so far. All right?

Barney I was imagining what could happen.

Jo Well please don't.

Barney You mean you haven't?

Jo We're not here to sit and dream about what *might* happen, what might be *if* . . . I keep my imagination in check.

Barney I wonder whether you've got one at all.

Jo I can think of worse deficiencies.

Barney You know, I often wonder if you're even human.

Ossie I thought we'd agreed not to waste time on rows?

Jo I'll be back.

(*The tent flap opens. Shriek of blizzard. Fades. Back inside the tent, three of the men are asleep. Heavy, rhythmic breathing. Barney is awake*)

Barney Ossie? Ossie? Are you awake? (*Pause*) Oh, hell. Chip? No. You're all bloody logs, you're all dreaming, look at you. Not that Jo dreams. He's got nothing in him to dream about. Tucked up in your little bags, look at you! (*He yawns. His voice grows drowsy*) The harder you try to sleep, the more you stay awake. So . . . the more you try to stay awake, you ought to go off to sleep. (*Pause*) 's logical.

(*Fade*)

Young Barney Go *on*, you said you'd go on.

Barney's Don't you know it by heart?
Mother

Young Barney Yes. But go on.

Barney's 'That same evening, after little Kay had gone home and was half
Mother undressed, he crept upon the chair by the window and peeped through the little round hole. Just then, a few snowflakes fell outside, and one of the largest of them remained lying on the edge of one of the flowerpots. The snowflake appeared larger and at last, took the form of a lady dressed in the finest white crêpe, her attire being composed of millions of starlike particles. She was exquisitely fair and delicate but entirely of ice; her eyes gleamed like two bright stars but there was no rest or repose in them. She nodded at the window and beckoned with her hand.' Barney . . . you're asleep.

Young Barney I'm *not*, I'm not, I'm . . .

(*Sudden shriek of wind. Barney comes awake*)

Barney I'm . . . No! No! (*Silence*) What? Ah . . . (*He lies back again*) Oh God. (*Blizzard outside*) Oh God help us. If you're out there. If you are. I don't know. (*Pause*) Ossie? Are you awake? Ossie? No, nobody's awake. I'm on my own. Alone. A-L-O-N-E. Only I'm not. I don't mind that. Not so much as going to sleep and meeting a nightmare half-way down the tunnel. Not dreams . . . nightmares. I always liked it . . . I always liked being alone, anywhere. Remember the day I went to Grandfather Percy's, and set off across the moors on my own and the mist came down and I found a sheep and sat by it. It kept me warm. It smelled sour. I wasn't afraid then. I think I was happy. It was what I wanted, so long as I could have the sheep for warmth, I was all right. The mist came right down, I could put out my hand and touch it. Damp. It was like a cobweb over my face. I didn't mind. They sent out a search party. God, they were the ones who were bothered, not me! Half killed me, Grandfather

Percy did . . . I was black and blue. I was only . . . what? Ten? Eleven? Something like that. I wonder why Harry wasn't with me. How old was he, then? No, wait a minute, I was nine, nine, and it was March, and Harry was in hospital, having his tonsils out. That's it! It's all coming back. Everything does, here. You lie and think and you're absolutely alone, and it all comes back. Perhaps that's what it's like when you're dying. I can close my eyes and they're all there . . . it hasn't changed, nothing's gone away at all. It's all there.

(His voice has become drowsy again. After a pause, the voice of his mother goes on reading)

Barney's 'The walls of the palace were formed of the driven snow, its
Mother doors and windows of the cutting winds. There were above a hundred halls, the largest of them many miles in extent, all illuminated by the Northern Lights; all alike, vast, empty, icily cold and dazzlingly white. No sounds of mirth ever resounded through these dreary spaces. No cheerful scene refreshed the sight. Vast, empty and cold were the Snow Queen's chambers, and the Northern Lights flashed, now high, now low, in regular graduation. In the midst of the empty, interminable snow-saloon lay a frozen lake. It was broken into a thousand pieces, but these pieces so exactly resembled each other that the breaking might well be deemed a work of more than human skill. The Snow Queen, when at home, always sat in the centre of this lake. She used to say that then she was sitting on the mirror of reason, and that hers was the best, indeed, the only one, in the world.'

(Voice fades into rising blizzard. Inside the tent. Ossie is whistling and banging tins)

Ossie Come on, porridge up! Come and get it . . . come on, out of it.

(Groans, mutters, movements of getting up)

Chip Do you know, I was dreaming about pineapples. Great fat slices of fresh pineapple dripping in sharp juice and covered in big dollops of thick, fresh yellow cream and . . . Ouch! *(Barney has thrown something at him)* All right, I just thought you'd find it interesting, that's all. You ought to be grateful to me. The only way we can get out of this hole, short of walking off into the blue beyond, is by dreaming . . . it's the least I can do, to share mine with everybody else, isn't it? What's *that*?

Ossie Porridge.

Chip It looks like . . .

Barney Chip!
> (*Chip mumbles. Begins to eat*)

Barney Where's Jo?

Ossie Gone out to look at the weather again.

Chip It's died down a bit.

Barney It was bloody terrible last night. Didn't you hear it?

Chip Never hear a thing, mate, from the moment my head touches the pillow. Sweet dreams, that's all! Did I tell you that when I'm at home, first thing every morning, my dog and I go for a tramp in the woods?

Ossie (*Taken in. Interested*) Oh yes?

Chip Yes. The dog enjoys it but the tramp's getting a bit fed up.
> (*Ossie groans. Howl of wind as Jo comes back in*)

Jo (*Stamping. Panting*) It's blown itself out, more or less. The sky's clear.

Chip Today's the day, tonight's the night then.

Jo Yes.

Barney Have you done the bits of paper?

Jo Yes. Put them in the tin.

Chip Pass the sugar over.

Ossie There's not much of that left.

Barney If the lot doesn't fall on you, Jo, are you going to have another go at the wireless?

Chip Moses was sick . . . and the lot fell on Aaron . . .

Jo Yes. I still think I might get something out of it.

Chip Never say die, all that sort of thing?

Jo Now look . . . listen . . . there's a lot of drift just as you get outside, the gale was blowing up this way. But once you're through that, you're onto the hard-packed stuff again, as far as I can tell. The thing is, to watch out that the fresh drift hasn't covered over crevasses. It looks to me as if whoever goes, should go South. Not North, South. If we're where we think we are, that is. From over there, on the far side of the Ridge, we might see something, now the weather's cleared.

Chip Such as?

Jo Some sign of the main party.

Barney They'll be miles away by now.

Jo We don't *know* that, we can't take it for granted. We can't take anything as read.

Barney I suppose not.

86

Jo I *know* not.

Ossie Any signs of them will have been obliterated by the downfall.

Jo Possibly . . . probably, but how do we know they aren't a mile or so over there, just on the other side? They've probably camped, like us. We've lost all sense of distance after three weeks of blizzard – so will they. It's even possible they may be sending out a reccy party for us. Well, isn't it? Look – have you all given *up*?

Barney Hadn't you better find that empty tin?

Jo Right.

Chip What's the fuel situation?

Jo Not good. Right, here's the tin, and here are the spills. (*Shaking it up*) I . . . I suppose nobody wants to opt out, do they? You might as well say now, if so. We're all prepared to go? It's risky, but not too risky, I should have said. I'm prepared to back my own judgement – that one of us ought to go out.

Chip Oh, get on with it.

Jo Right. Barney – you pick first.

(*Ossie starts to sing the following 'round'. The others gradually join in*)

'London's burning, London's burning,
Bring the engine, bring the engine,
Fire, fire! Fire, fire!
Pour on water, pour on water.'

(*In the middle, at a point when they are all singing, Jo stops*)

Jo I've got it. (*The others stop dead*) It's here.

Chip That's it then. You're the one to go.

Jo Yes.

(*Fade*)

(*Fade up, Jo is ready for off*)

Barney All right, then, Jo – you've got the compass?

Chip That's a laugh for a start.

Jo Oh hell, these bloody gloves have got a hole in them. Lend me yours, Ossie, they're the nearest size.

Ossie Right.

Chip You've got the flares? That's the most important thing.

Jo Yes. I've got the lot now.

Chip Right, well don't forget to send us a postcard to say you've arrived safely.

Jo You're not to think of forming any search party for four hours at least, is that clear? There'd be no point. It'll be slow going, it's very deep out there now.

Barney Look – are you sure one of us oughtn't to go with you?

Jo We've been through all that. We've decided.

Barney All the same . . .

Chip He's afraid you might get a bit lonely, see?

Jo We're wasting time.

Ossie Are those gloves all right?

Jo Yes, fine thanks. Right then.

Chip Here, don't just go off like that. We want to come and wave you goodbye. Do you know, when a ship leaves dock, they have paper streamers held by passengers on the deck at one end, and the people standing on the quay at the other, and they unravel as the ship moves off. (*Pause*) And then they break. Oh well, it was a thought.

Jo You would have tried to get them laughing on the *Titanic* wouldn't you?

Chip Now don't let's get carried away, you're only going for a little toddle down the road, to see how the penguins are mating.

Jo See you later.

Barney Good luck, Jo.

Chip (*Calling*) Got your Union Jack have you?

Barney He's all right, you know – Jo . . . he's not a bad bloke.

Chip Save the obituary notices, you might need them later.

Ossie Get that flap shut, it's bloody freezing in here.

Barney I suppose he'll be all right . . .

Ossie Oh come on, he knows what he's doing, he'll be O.K. Stop fidgeting.

> (*He starts to play the guitar. Fade*)
> (*Fade up. The wind keening faintly. The first two verses of the 'Lyke-Wake Dirge' sung as though on the wind. Song fades. Jo's footsteps, plunging about in the snow. Frequent pauses. His breathing heavy. He grunts, murmurs. His voice becomes more confused and slurred during the speech. The weather worsens*)

Jo That's it . . . the thing is . . . to know . . . where you're going . . . exactly . . . where I am going . . . steady . . . watch out for cracks . . . look before you leap . . . good motto of a . . . sensible man . . . I'm a sensible man . . . Oh God . . . it's a slap in the face . . . They ought at least to show you the goods . . . they ought to let you have them on approval . . . it's this . . . this

isn't what I meant . . . Oh God, it was going to be . . . listen,
I'm a *brave man* . . . I know . . . I'm . . . I can't see . . . but this
isn't what I meant . . . Well, you are stuck with it, old boy, you
are hoist with your own . . . what? Out here, by yourself . . .
Oh, Jesus, I'm frightened when they leave me by myself . . .
don't put the light out . . . don't draw the curtains . . . stay with
me . . . But I wanted to come . . . it means . . . well, this is why.
It's all here. On your own. All right? You've been there . . .
you've found them . . . and back, right? This is what they write
about, this sort of . . . you've found them and back . . . one . . .
two . . . three . . . four . . . five. (*He trips and falls flat*)
Hell. You want to look where you're going. Hell . . . Oh God,
I can't see the tent, *I can't see the tent* . . . it's here, it must be
here . . . it's . . . Oh God, It's . . . of course it's here . . . of course
you can see the tent, don't be so bloody silly. You've come out
one mile, one mile, they were no more than a mile off, due
South, straight ahead . . . and now you're coming back . . . it's
all right . . . due South, I said . . . Of course you . . . all right,
then, all right . . . their bodies were frozen stiff. I'm frozen . . .
stiff . . . Oh, God, I always used to say . . . All right, shut up,
think about it . . . think . . . get your bearings . . . This is what
happens . . . it's snowing again . . . Oh, Jesus Christ . . .

   (*Fade*)
   (*In the tent. Ossie is playing the mouth-organ*)

Chip What time is it?
Barney You ask that every five minutes . . . you keep on asking.
Chip It's gone darker, as well.
   (*Ossie stops playing*)
Barney It's three o'clock.
Chip Right . . . who goes out, who stays?
Barney We haven't seen the flare go up.
Chip He might be lying somewhere and too injured to send it off. He
   might be unconscious. It was bloody silly for one man to go on
   his own. Bloody ridiculous.
Barney He told us to wait four hours. He said . . . don't do anything
   before four hours.
Ossie How long is it?
Chip Three.
Barney He wasn't reckoning on a change of weather then.
Ossie We none of us were.

89

Chip All right . . . what do we do? Go? Or wait?

Barney Ossie?

Ossie Wait.

Barney Chip?

Chip (*Hesitates*) Wait . . . I think.

Barney Two to one. All right, we wait. Fancy a game of cards?

Chip What I can't understand is how we came to be stuck with SNAP. Bloody hell, it's not even HAPPY FAMILIES. Who put SNAP in there in the first place?

Barney Are you playing or not?

Chip Not.

Barney Right then.

(*Ossie resumes the mouth-organ tune*)

We've only got to sit in here and wait.

Chip Can't you think of another tune?

(*Fade*)

(*Outside in the blizzard. Jo is blundering about wildly. Sings snatches of a song . . .*)

Jo Joseph . . . Joseph . . . is my name . . .

My friends all call me . . . Jo . . .

I'm up, you know . . . to every . . . game . . .

And . . . everything . . . I . . . know . . .

And I . . . was green as green could be . . .

I suffered . . . for it . . . though . . .

Now, if they . . . try it on with . . . me, I . . .

tell them . . . not . . . for . . . Jo . . .

(*He trips. Falls. Lies sobbing*)

Oh, Jesus, I can't feel where my . . . hands are . . . Where are they? . . . Oh, God . . . God, why don't you stop this . . . bloody snow? If you're supposed to be . . . GOD . . . why don't you make it stop . . . what the hell are you . . . there for?

(*He breaks down into wild sobbing*)

(*Fade up. Inside the tent. Mouth-organ playing*)

Chip Heads or tails?

Barney Tails.

Chip It's heads. Again.

Barney Tails.

Chip Heads. You shouldn't put all your eggs in one basket – that's your trouble you know. You owe me sixteen toffees and I'll have nut ones. Heads or tails?

Barney Balls.

Chip I say, I say, I say, what was wrong with the cross-eyed teacher?
(*Barney punches him hard on the jaw. Silence. Ossie breaks off the mouth-organ music abruptly*)

Chip (*Cool*) Well – you speak your mind, Barney, I'll say that for you.

Barney I . . . I didn't mean to hit you.

Chip O.K.

Barney Look . . .

Chip I said O.K. And what the bloody hell are *you* sitting there for, with your eyes out like chapel hat-pegs?

Ossie Sorry. (*Plays mouth-organ again*)

Chip Oh, Christ, not that again, I can't stand it.
(*Abrupt silence*)

Barney Anyway, what *was* wrong with him?

Chip Who?

Barney The cross-eyed teacher.

Chip Oh. (*Uninterested*) He had no control over his pupils.

Ossie (*Urgent*) I can hear something.
(*He opens the tent flap. Wind roars. Jo's crying, behind*)

Chip Barney, get the lamp. Ossie, start up the primus. What do you two know about first aid?

Barney Not enough.
(*Outside. Blizzard and gale. They shout over it*)

Chip I can't see a bloody thing.

Barney I can still hear something. Listen . . .
(*Wind moans. Jo's cry*)

Ossie It is him. Over there. No, the other way . . . No . . .

Chip The gale's blowing his voice . . . it's blowing ours as well, he won't know where we are.

Ossie There he is . . . not far . . .

Chip He's almost on top of us, dammit . . .

Ossie He's covered in snow, he's half buried in it. I couldn't see him at all . . .

Barney God, look at him . . .

Chip He's alive.

Barney Only just. He should never have gone.

Chip Come on, Jo, we've got you . . . Oh, Christ, he's frozen stiff, it's frozen to his face . . . we'll have to hack him out . . .

Ossie Let's shut up and get him inside, shall we? All right, Jo.
(*Jo moans incessantly. Sound of them digging. Pulling*)

Chip Get his legs . . . it's like dragging a load of lead . . . what in God's name happened? He'll never be able to tell us, by the look of him. He's been wandering for hours, round and round.

Ossie Shut up and take his weight.

> (*Fade*)
> (*Inside the tent. Jo moans softly*)

Ossie What's he saying, Chip?

Chip Nothing. He's mumbling to himself. I don't know what.

Barney He doesn't know where he is. Look at him . . .

> (*Fade into Jo's delirium. Children running about in a playground. Jo's sister's voice, close to us*)

Sister Jo-ey . . . Jo-ey . . . Jo-ey . . .

Young Jo I told you to shut up and go away, this is a thing for boys, it's not a girl's game and we don't want girls here.

Sister What is it?

Jo It's an important war. That's a city and it's going to be stormed and sacked. Go away.

Sister You're supposed to be looking after me. I'm supposed to stay with you all the time, she said so.

Jo If you don't go away from me and stop spoiling this game, I'll make you sorry, that's all. I don't like you.

Sister I don't know what else to do.

Jo Go and feed the ducks.

Sister What with?

Jo Grass.

Sister Ducks don't eat grass, stupid.

Jo How do you know? You haven't tried have you?

Sister I don't want to.

Jo Go *on*.

Sister I've got to stay with you.

Jo I'll make you go, I'll twist your arm off.

> (*He grabs her. They are moving towards the lake. Sound speeded up and distorted*)

You're going to do as I say. I'll push you into the water.

Sister Let me go . . . no, no, no, no, no, no . . .

Jo Do as I say . . . do, as I say, as I say, as I say, as . . .

> (*A scream. A splash. They merge together, inside Jo's head, into a single piercing sound. Then the adult Jo calls out of the sound, and his delirium*)

Jo That's what they looked like . . . there they are . . . there they . . .

I mean . . . dead . . . I saw . . . dead and I saw . . . they were frozen and alive and drowning . . . dead . . . Oh, God . . .

Chip Does he mean the others? Is that what he means?

Barney You can't tell.

Chip Well, there's nothing we can do.

Barney He still isn't warm enough.

Ossie He keeps saying they were frozen stiff . . . they were dead.

Chip Well, he might have seen anything, anything at all . . . he might have been delirious and seen nothing. How long had he been lying out there?

(*Jo groans. Mutters. Goes into a delirium again*)

Woman (*Calling*) Jo-eeee . . . Jo-eeee.

Jo No, no, no . . . Oh God, it wasn't my fault . . . no . . .

Chip Try and give him another drink.

Barney How? You've only got to look at him . . .

Chip Well, what *else* can we do, for Christ's sake?

Barney Sit with him. Wait. There's nothing else, is there?

Chip (*Hysterical*) And what if he dies? What then?

Barney (*Quietly*) We're all dying. Aren't we?

(*Fade*)

(*Fade up. Later. Jo's rattling breathing is heard*)

Barney How is he?

Chip Worse, I think. He looks worse.

Barney Does he need anything?

Chip There's nothing we can give him if there is. We've just got to wait.

Barney I'm sick of bloody waiting. We've waited the last month. I feel as if I've been waiting all my life.

Chip Tell us a joke then, Ossie, cheer us all up.

Ossie That's your department.

Chip I've run out.

Barney What are you reading, Ossie?

Ossie Oh, 'improving literature'. Nothing up your street.

Barney How the hell do you know? Here, do you remember at the first base camp, how Ted and Lomas used to read *Alice in Wonderland* aloud in turns? I liked that. Sent me right off the sleep it did.

Chip Read to us then, Ossie, improve us. We could do with it.

Barney We don't want to disturb Jo.

Chip No, he can't hear us. He's too far gone.

Barney He sounds worse.

93

Chip   Go on, Ossie. We need taking out of ourselves.

Ossie   You won't want to hear this.

Barney   Is it the only book we've got with us?

Ossie   Yes. Or the prayer book.

Chip   Then we'll have what you've got.

Ossie   All right. (*Reads*) 'It is a barbarous part of inhumanity to add unto any afflicted party's misery or endeavour to multiply in any man a passion whose single nature is already above his patience. This was the greatest affliction of Job, and those oblique expostulations of his friends a deeper injury than the downright blows of the Devil. It is not the tears of our own eyes only, but of our friends' also, that do exhaust the current of our sorrows; which, falling into many streams, runs more peaceably and is contented with a narrower channel. It is an act within the power of charity to translate a passion out of one breast into another, and to divide a sorrow almost out of itself; for an affliction, like a dimension, may be so divided as, if not indivisible, at least to become insensible. Now with my friend, I desire not to share or to participate but to engross his sorrows; that by making them mine own, I may more easily discuss them; for in my own reason, and within myself, I can command that which I cannot entreat without myself, and within the circle of another.'

    (*During the last words, Jo's breathing has stopped*)

Barney   Ossie . . .

    (*Silence*)

Chip   He's dead.

Barney   Yes.

Chip   I didn't notice. A man lies in the same tent with you and dies and you don't notice.

Barney   What do we do now, then?

Ossie   We bury him.

    (*Outside. Gale. Spades digging in the snow*)

Ossie   (*Reading*) 'Man that is born of woman hath but a short time to live and is full of misery. He cometh up and is cut down like a flower; he fleeth as it were a shadow and never continueth in one stay. In the midst of life we are in death . . .' (*Fade*)

    (*Fade up. The tent*)

Barney   . . . Got five bob for it at Ikey Sykes, the jeweller. That seemed like money! He never found any more. He used to bring stones home, pocketsful of stones, but that's all they ever were – stones.

Then my grandmother started us on making rugs – rag rugs, woollen rugs . . . we'd make them and sell them. We did too, but we never made more than a few bob profit. I tell you what, it's been reminding me of that, us being in here, it's like the evenings we spent sitting round the fire, each one of us working on his own corner of the rug. There was something very companionable about that. Then we'd have cocoa at nine o'clock, and Harry and I were sent to bed.

Chip   The cocoa's finished.

Barney   It was cold then, as well, in that farm cottage – freeze your face off when you opened the back door.

Chip   There's no comparison.

Barney   You wouldn't know.

Chip   Bloody stuck here, three of us left, waiting to see which runs out first, the food or the fuel, so that we know if we're going to freeze to death or starve.

Ossie   There's no point in talking about it.

Chip   Aren't you human? Aren't you scared to the guts about it? Because I am, I'll tell you that, I am. I never did like the idea of death much. Well now it's grinning over my shoulder, I like it even less. I'm a coward Ossie. Got it?

Ossie   I'll make us a drink.

Chip   The cocoa's *finished*.

Ossie   Oh – yes. Well, there's tea. A spoon or two of tea.

Chip   We buried a man out there! Don't you understand that? One man is lying and rotting under those great thick slabs of frozen snow, and he's the first of us. Who's next? I didn't even like Jo, and that makes it worse. Not better – worse. Who's next? Don't you ask yourself that?

Barney   There's no point.

Ossie   Anyway, you don't rot. Not at that temperature.

(*Chip yells out suddenly and hysterically. Barney hits him. He stops*)

Chip   How many more times are you going to hit me?

Barney   Tell us a joke, why can't you? Sing a song, do a dance . . . what's *happened* to you?

Chip   I've started to think. I thought – what if I'm the one who's left, if I have to dig the graves in the snow and if I take a long, long time to die in here, by myself, or if I go mad? I always was afraid of going mad. I used to wake up in the middle of the night and not know who I was and think I was going mad. My father went mad. Did I . . . did I tell you about my father? He kept a joke shop. Jokes and magic. Equipment for conjurors, masks, itching powder, rubber spiders, stink-bombs . . . you name it. Used to do a lot of his business by mail order. But in the end, he went mad. He went beserk with a carving knife one night, and after they put him away, he would sit, day after day, on a stool, in the middle of the room, without any clothes on. He didn't know any of us. And he used to sing. He'd sing hymns and music hall songs . . . and then he'd cry. Oh, I hated that. I couldn't stand it. Have you ever seen a man of fifty, with tears streaming down his face, crying like a baby? He didn't bother to stop, or wipe them off, or anything. He just cried. Then he'd try to do injuries to himself, and if he couldn't lay his hands on a pair of scissors or a knife, he'd scratch himself with his nails and when they cut his nails, he sank his teeth into his own flesh. He didn't die for years, eight or nine years, and we had to go and see him every week and he never knew who we were, so where was the point? I had to put my best suit on, to go and see him. The collar rubbed my neck raw. Well, don't you think I expect all that to happen to me? Only out here, there are no nurses, no locked doors . . . just thousands of miles of ice and snow to go mad in. Think about it, you two, go on. What else is there to think about?

Ossie I'll tell you. There are two flares left, and there might, or there might not be the rest of the party, somewhere out there, dead or alive, and there might be rescue planes coming out, now the weather's changed again. Are we going to send a flare up? Is one of us going off to look for the others? Did Jo find them, frozen to death, is that what he was talking about?

Chip You've bloody taken over from him . . . little Master of Ceremonies. Talk loud enough and fast enough and you won't hear the sound of the screaming inside your own head.

Ossie It's too late to do anything today. We'll eat and sleep and start up again tomorrow.

Chip (*Sings*) 'And if one green bottle, should accidentally fall, there'd be two green bottles hanging on the wall.'

Barney Who's going to cook?

Chip There is, of course, always the question of suicide.

Barney How many tins of meat left?

Ossie Eight. No cocoa. Half a packet of tea. Quite a lot of beans.

Chip Don't you love me any more? Why aren't you talking to me?

Hey – have you put me in the corner?

Ossie No.

Chip Do I make you nervous? I think Barney's going to punch me again. It's a habit he's got into. Ah – see that shifty look come into his eyes? Oh yes. Well, I'll tell you, I've been thinking. Very seriously, and I've been wondering what in hell we thought we'd get out of this place, and do you know, I can't answer you? Aren't we using all this business of physical endurance simply in order to avoid confronting the truth? Truth about what, you may ask, and I can't answer you there, either . . . we haven't got around to it yet. Truth inside us, or outside of us? Just so long as we bother about the fuel running out and whether we can keep our socks dry and how many flares there are left, we avoid any serious confrontation with it. Do you know what they tell those who are recently bereaved, to prevent them from coming face to face with the truth? They say, keep busy, give yourself too much to do, take your mind off it. And that's what we've done. We've all of us been so damned busy for the last four months, seeing how far we can go. Mad mesomorphs, that's us.

Ossie Are you going to lie there on your back for the rest of the day?

Chip Have you a better suggestion? Do you know, Ossie, the little Hitler is coming out in you?

Ossie What about those weather reports?

Chip Oh, I can give you those from here. Saves all that bother with little charts and meters. 'Snow, snow and more snow, temperatures anything up to fifty degrees below freezing . . . and what's a variation of ten degrees between friends? Outlook – no change.'

Barney Oh, leave him alone, for God's sake, you won't get any sense out of him at the moment.

Chip Is it sense we're so greatly in need of, in our present hour of crisis then? (*Silence. Clatter of plates*) Oh, pardon me for breathing, will you? (*Silence*) All *right*, here we go. Barney, what did the two blood cells do?

Barney Lived in vein.

Chip Thank you. Ossie, why is Sunday the strongest day?

Ossie Because all the other days are weak days.

Chip Barney, why does lightning shock people?

Barney I don't know, Chip, why does lightning shock people?

Chip Because it doesn't know how to conduct itself.

(*Barney laughs shortly. Chip begins to laugh hysterically*)

Barney O.K. O.K.

Ossie That's enough.

Barney All right, Chip.

    (*Chip goes on laughing more loudly*)

Ossie Chip, shut up, the joke's over. Get a hold of yourself.

Barney It wasn't that funny.

Ossie Chip, what . . .

Barney Put that ice-axe down, what the hell do you think you're doing?

Ossie Chip, don't be such a bloody fool, leave him alone . . .

    CHIP!

Barney No! (*Yells. A thud*)

Ossie Oh, Jesus . . .

    (*Chip's laughter dies to a hysterical whimper*)

Chip What . . . what's happened?

Ossie Oh, Jesus Christ!

Chip What did I do that for, Ossie? What did I hit him for? What happened, Ossie . . . *what did I do?*

Ossie Killed him. That's what you did. You killed him.

Chip Oh, God, he's bleeding all over, look, he's . . .

Ossie Dead, Chip. Dead.

    (*Outside. Blizzard. A single spade, choppng into snow. Fades. Inside the tent again. Chip wakes. Stirs*)

Chip Ossie? Ossie?

Ossie (*Alarmed*) What's the matter?

Chip Listen, I killed Barney. I killed him. How in God's name can you just lie there and sleep?

Ossie I don't know. I seem to be able to. I suppose . . . because I know it won't happen again.

Chip No. (*Pause*) You ought to put me on trial, Ossie. You ought to convict me and sentence me and carry out the punishment. 'I'll be judge, I'll be jury, said cunning old fury, I'll try the whole cause and condemn you to death.' Is that right?

Ossie Something like.

Chip Funny, remembering that. Well . . . why don't you do it?

Ossie Chip, there's no point in going on about it. It's all done with. Everything's done with.

Chip You don't care much either, do you?

Ossie Not much.

Chip I've never been a violent man . . . I've never . . . you know, done anything . . . hit anyone or . . . I mean, I've always been careful about things like that. I don't like to see people boxing, people slapping their kids. I wouldn't smack a dog over the nose with a newspaper, not like some people do. Look . . . I couldn't stand Jo, none of us could . . . but Barney . . . I *liked* Barney, didn't I? You know that. He was my friend. We're all . . . what's happened to me, Ossie?

Ossie I think it's what's been happening to all of us.

Chip You haven't tried to kill anyone.

Ossie No. But we've all behaved like different people, haven't we? The people we thought we were somehow got lost, or else we got out of touch with them. And new people emerged. We didn't know them. We didn't know anyone.

Chip But *why*?

Ossie I think . . . look . . . what kind of people were we, all of us – tough guys, wasn't that right? That's what we saw ourselves as really. We didn't get scared. We *did* things. We didn't think much. Even Barney didn't. He daydreamed, that's all. It's all surface. We're physical men. We thought we were brave men. Jo did. I did. You did – you're an army man. Barney did that rock-climbing, when he was only about ten, hanging off a sheer cliff-face at the end of a rope. That's what we were all like, that's why we came here. We can do it. It doesn't matter what goes wrong, we'll find a way out, because that is what we are like and if we don't . . . we'll face the facts squarely. So . . . we thought it would always be like that. But we didn't know a thing, not one bloody thing . . . about ourselves, or about each other, we'd never had to get below the skin of anybody before. There was always the next place to move on to, the next job to do. Then . . . suddenly, here we are, the four of us. Dead end country. Nothing to do. No point in getting on with the next job, it wouldn't lead anywhere. So, we sat and looked at each other for the first time. We'd never done that before. Never had to cope with how different we all might turn out to be from the guys we thought we were. Never had to go by instinct. And we couldn't do it, could we, Chip? I went on singing songs, because that's a way of getting out. You went on cracking corny jokes. Jo went on *doing* things, fiddling with that bloody radio, getting himself frozen to death in that bloody useless expedition. Barney went on day-dreaming. Only it hasn't worked. In the end, we can't stay behind the smoke screen, can we? In the end, there's you and there is me, and there's waiting to die. Not knowing. And being scared as all get out. Bloody terrified. That's what I am. We're not like Scott's crew, are we? We've been comparing ourselves with them. We'd write a last line, telling them to look after the folks back home, and turn our faces to the wall and wait composedly for brother Death ... dignified, heroic, courageous, believing. But we failed. No one will ever know it, but we have failed. I don't know if it matters. We've been acting out a little puppet show for ourselves. We're not brave, we're cowards, there's nothing special about us, this is the time we haven't won. We wish we had never bloody come here, we want to wake up and find out it was all a nasty dream. But it wasn't. It isn't. We're here, Chip, that's all. It's been the truth at the back of our minds the whole time, hasn't it?

Chip So – what *did* we come here for?

Ossie Because the men we thought we were had a pretty good selection of reasons . . . all the usual; challenge, endurance, toughening up, discovery . . . all that. But the whole system broke down. The men we really *are* didn't want to come at all, and they can't cope with it now they're here. They've been led on. Conned. Like a Jack o'Lantern, leading men into bogs and ditches in the darkness.

Chip So what's the answer?

Ossie Oh, there is no answer, is there? Not now. Not for us. We should have found out the truth before we came. But the paradox is that we couldn't find out the truth *until* we came. So there you are.

Chip Rats in a trap.

Ossie Barney and Jo are dead.

Chip We'll be dead. Sooner or later.

Ossie Sooner.

Chip Yes.

(*Ossie begins to play his guitar softly. When they talk again, their tone has changed. They are back on the surface*)

Chip Why didn't you ever get married?

Ossie I never fancied it. Not my cup of tea. I like my own company.

Chip Dead or alive?

Ossie Something like that.

Chip Is that why you came out here with us?

Ossie It's a thing you've got to cure yourself of – liking your own company too much. It's not very healthy.

Chip But being married is the good life . . . having a family . . . it keeps out the cold on winter nights.

Ossie Not in the end, it doesn't.

Chip No.

Ossie In the end, nothing does. In the end, you're on your own.

Chip For better – or worse.

Ossie Yep.

Chip Do you believe in hell, Ossie?

Ossie I used to.

Chip Because what they tell you about it isn't true – they tell you it's all flames and fire, they tell you you're burned to the bone. So you are, but not fire-burn. *Ice* burn. It's the cold that kills you, boy, the bitter freezing cold.

Ossie (*Plays guitar and sings softly*)
'And then we came to that cold country,
 Where the ice and snow do lie,
 Where there's ice and snow,
 And the great whales blow,
 And the long night does not die.'

Chip I killed a man. *I killed Barney.* (*Pause*) Put the lamp on. Let's have a light while we can. A lighted road to death.
  (*Movement. Match strikes*)
 It sends out shadows like fingers.

Ossie Did you ever make shadow puppets on the walls?

Chip Yes! A rabbit . . . like that?

Ossie Yes. And a church. No, no . . . first two fingers. That's it. What else?

Chip A fox.

Ossie A crippled man.

Chip The Devil – look – great black devil up on the wall. Ah – I know you!

Ossie 'Dance devil, dance,
 In a ring, in a ring,
 A dance with death
 As the King, as the King.'

Chip You get used to it, Ossie, it . . .

Ossie Yes.

Chip I'm just . . . *tired.* (*Pause*) Where did you learn to play music?

Ossie Just picked it up. I took the guitar to Brazil once. It's a meal ticket – I did well. I went down a long, black river through the jungle. It was bloody hot.

Chip You've been around. Looking for – a bolt-hole, was that what you said?

Ossie Somewhere. Something to pull over my head. Keep out the cold.

Chip (*Laughs*) Is it like you thought it would be – that place?

Ossie Yes – in a way. I'm not surprised, now I'm here. Not now I'm here.

> (*He plucks the guitar again. Chip begins to move about the tent, putting on clothes*)

Chip (*At the tent-flap*) It's nice ... that tune.

Ossie Yes.

Chip Don't come out after me.

Ossie No.

Chip No.

> (*Gale and blizzard roar as the tent flap opens and he goes out. Fade. The last two verses of the 'Lyke-Wake Dirge'. Then the wind and blizzard take over*)

Consider the Lilies

Consider the Lilies was first broadcast on BBC Radio 3
on 18 September 1973, with the following cast:

LESAGE	*Vernon Joyner*
MRS LESAGE	*Betty Huntley-Wright*
YOUNG BOWMAN	*Nicholas Dillane*
LOTTIE	*Julie Hallam*
BOWMAN	*Tony Britton*
DOCTOR	*Clive Swift*
NURSE	*Diana Olsson*
SUSANNAH	*Helen Worth*

The music was specially composed for this production by Geoffrey Burgon and performed by:

Doreen Price (Soprano)
John York Skinner (Counter-Tenor)
Nona Liddell (Violin)
Geoffrey Burgon (Celeste)
David Corkhill (Vibraphone)
John Marson (Harp)

Produced by Guy Vaesen.

(Music and the chorus of plants. A male and a female chorus, set on either speaker. They are separate at the beginning, and join together towards the end, when the music becomes reminiscent of the music which will later 'blossom out' into the visionary theme)

Chorus 1	Chorus 2
Cinnabar	Destiny
Croesus	Enchantment
Harmony	Prosperity
Ruby	Discovery
Citronella	Mercury
Sonata	Jupiter

Together

Queen of the Night

Black Dragon	Black Beauty
Green Dragon	Clarion
Heart's Desire	Apollo
Royal Gold	Verona

Empress of China

Empress of India   Empress of Japan

Lilies of the Field

Lesage I took a good look at him today – his eyes. I really wanted to get a good look at his eyes. It was a theory I had.

Mrs L Eat your soup.

Lesage Dilated. That's the thing to look out for. The pupils of the eyes go dilated.

Mrs L You'd a squint when you were just over two. A definite squint. Your left eye used to wander. That's what it's called – or lazy, a lazy eye. Worried me. It was in the air raid shelter one night, we'd just got down there.

(Lesage groans)

We were in for a real night of it, you got a sixth sense about things in those days. Like a telepathy. We knew when we were going to get a real pasting from Jerry. *And* we did. It was Mrs Pennyhackett from number 24. You won't remember her, of course. She had a nasty thrombosis. You were only six then, or seven – yes, seven. You won't remember.

Lesage No.

Mrs L She spotted it. Your eye. I never liked her. She was a mite too sharp, too – well, I wouldn't say superior, no, but she liked to tell you what you didn't know, liked to be one up. 'Squint', she said, straight away, soon as we'd got down there that night, after the sirens went. 'Squint'. Well, it was all right for those like her without responsibilities, but there I was, trying to get you settled, get you under the blankets before the fireworks went up. I wasn't paying much attention. But she went on. Turned you round, peered into your eyes.

Lesage She had hairs coming out of little moles on her chin.

Mrs L You wouldn't remember her.

Lesage Little black bristly hairs.

Mrs L You were only two. Anyway, she took a good look, and of course, then *I* had to. And she was right. Oh, yes, I'm sorry to say it, but she was quite right. 'Very observant' I told her. You'd a squint. A definite cast in your left eye.

Lesage It wandered.

Mrs L I panicked. I thought, here we go, hospitals, doctors, operations, pain, the child parted from his mother *and* in war-time.

Lesage And me only two.

Mrs L I whistled you round there the next day. Old Doctor Macrae it was then, nice, old-fashioned family man, brought you into the world – did his own dispensing in a cubby-hole round the back.

Lesage Yellow medicine, thick as syrup and tasting of tin. Great fat bottles.

Mrs L And he sent us to the hospital. It was a right caper, I can tell you and the place half boarded up, with the glass having been blown out of the windows and beds in three rows down every ward and casualties arriving as fast as the ambulances could get through.

Lesage Do you ever remember 1928, say, or 1953, or last year? What *was* it about the war?

Mrs L Atropine, they called it. Funny stuff.

Lesage 'A poisonous alkaloid found in the plant atropa belladonna – deadly nightshade.'

Mrs L You know them all!

Lesage Causes the pupils to dilate.

Mrs L In a little metal tube. They put it in your eye and we had to wait half an hour. Gave them a better view, I suppose. Then examined your eyes under a microscope.

Lesage Ophthalmoscope.

Mrs L Worried me.

Lesage I've got perfect eyesight, always had. I spotted the first shoot on a new japonica aureoreticulata at 75 yards.

Mrs L Time, they said. Just a question of the eye muscles strengthening themselves with time. No operation, not even a pair of those spectacles with one eye plastered out.

Lesage I always wanted those.

Mrs L It would right itself, they said, *and* it did.

Lesage Georgie Harding had one, for a year, more than a year, made him look like Captain Hook. I envied him those spectacles.

Mrs L So now he's been taking drugs has he? Nothing would surprise me.

Lesage Drugs?

Mrs L You said he'd got dilated pupils. Sure sign.

Lesage I said I looked to see if he had. I examined his eyes. I had a theory.

Mrs L A man of his age and position.

Lesage Not drugs.

Mrs L There are some funny people about. You aren't happy with the way he runs that job, are you?

Lesage It was illness I was on the lookout for, the first signs of something . . . well, he isn't right, is he? Why is he acting so peculiar? Why is he miles away, in a trance, half the time? Why doesn't he seem interested in what's under his nose? New plans, buildings that need renovating, new arrangements to be discussed for next spring's display beds, the floral clock? He lives in a world of his own. He doesn't seem to . . . the lilies, of course, he takes all that interest in those lilies, they might be his children . . . Well, very nice, all to the good, I'm fond of a well-set-up lily myself.

Mrs L Funny you never got hay-fever. Your cousin Frank's boys all had hay-fever, couldn't go near grass or pollen, couldn't so much as be in the same room as a vase of flowers, and you can imagine what that meant, with Frank running the wreaths and funeral sprays side of the business. It reminded me, you mentioning lilies. They were evacuated to a farm in Kent, right at the start, in 1939, when we thought it was all under way from the beginning. All of them together. They couldn't stand it. It was the hops. Had to stop indoors. Didn't know which was worse in the end, hops or bombs. Funny that. You never got it and it was on your father's side. And then you, out of the blue, going in for botany.

Lesage I tell you what I think then, if he isn't ill, he's got some hidden worries. Something . . .

Mrs L What worries can he have? Well-off bachelor, height of his profession, all those men working under him, secretary of this and that society, nice comfortable house, no family ties.

Lesage He could be lonely.

Mrs L He ought to find himself a nice wife then. He's no right to let his personal problems interfere with his work. He's no right to stand in your way, either.

Lesage I wish I could . . . I'd like to talk to him . . . open him out a bit. I've worked under him for – what – five years . . .

Mrs L Six come January.

Lesage Been promoted three times, he must think something of me. He might be a different species, do you know that? He might have come from another planet. I don't understand what goes on in his mind. I'd like to find out. I mean . . . look at what we've got in common. Plants, flowers, the whole botanical gardens, the whole organisation . . . I could talk to him about my plans for a research programme into carnivorous plants. I could . . . I don't know. I can't seem to find a way through. We never meet. He lives in another world.

Mrs L It's not right, you're young, you've ambitions. You always liked plants, even from a little boy. You made a beautiful garden in a kitchen saucer when you were only three, the afternoon before those four houses in Albany Street got a direct hit, and not so much as a warning, not a peep were we given out of that siren, crash-bang, while I was peeling the potatoes, I thought the world was coming to an end.

Lesage I still have dreams about that. The noise.

Mrs L You were too young to remember. And there you'd been, making that lovely garden, all neat, it was, all orderly, little paths marked out with rows of pebbles, bits of twig and so on, just like a proper laid-out public park.

Lesage I've plans in my head for a new aroid house as well, did I tell you? I could get them down on paper, a few tentative sketches. I'd like to draw him in, I'd like to discuss it with him. Well, I've no authority to proceed on my own, have I? Major changes, demolition, modernisation, experimentation? Where can I go without his say-so? Not a step, not a step. Does he want the gardens to stay in the age they were built, does he want the standard of research and plant-care to be on a par with the Victorians? I *am* his number 2. I am his assistant. You'd think I was the man who sweeps up the leaves for all the collaboration there is. He just doesn't seem interested. It isn't as if I didn't like him. If I understood him at all. It isn't as if I thought he'd got it in for me. I don't think he sees it, how frustrating it is, working all on my own, having no support from above, looking at him and he's miles away, dreaming about something or other.

Mrs L   Have you finished eating? I want to get off in time.

Lesage   Off?

Mrs L   Upholstery class. Tuesdays is upholstery. Not that there's much in it. I mean, I go for the company as much as anything, don't I? Only nobody seems very friendly, do you know what I mean? People all tucked up inside themselves. There isn't the camaraderie there was, we've lost that. There isn't all the give and take and time for chat like we had in the air-raid shelters.

(*Lesage hums 'Keep the Home Fires Burning'*)

You can laugh, but it was a great support, it was what kept us all going, kept us together and cheerful. You were too young, and your father overseas, what else had I? But everyone mucked in, we were all pals together. It's different now.

Lesage   Every man for himself.

Mrs L   I like to have my friends. I like to have a chat.

Lesage   Don't forget your big needle.

Mrs L   I still can't get ITV and they promised to come yesterday, they still haven't come, I've fiddled with it all the afternoon. That's another thing you can't rely on these days, service from shops, it isn't what it was.

Lesage   I don't want to watch, I've got work to do, I've got a plan to draw up. I had some ideas about that area over by the North Temperate house, beyond the pergola. We don't use that half enough. It's got potential, that area. A maze, that's what I'd like to see, a proper maze, privet or yew. Of course it'd take some years to grow up, even if we planted mature stock but it'd be an attraction, it'd be a feature. I'm going to design a maze. Not that it'll come to anything. Bowman won't be interested, he won't even be listening. He'll pick up the paper and stare through it. What's he staring at, that's what I'd like to know. What's he seeing?

(*Music*)
(*Song set to high soprano and harp*)
The blessed damozel leaned out
From the gold bar of heaven.
Her eyes were deeper than the depth
Of waters stilled at even.
She had three lilies in her hand
And the stars in her hair were seven.
(*Fade*)
(*Children's voices. Bowman, as a boy, and his sister Lottie*)

Young Father, father, come here. Come quickly. Oh, why won't father
Bowman come?
Lottie He's asleep.
Young B Under the paper.
Lottie He's going pink. Pink as a lobster.
Young B Under the newspaper he couldn't have seen.
Lottie Seen what?
Young B Everything falling.
Lottie What was falling?
Young B You saw it. Falling into the sea. Everything.
Lottie What are you talking about? There wasn't anything falling.
Young B Yes, there was a silver cloud and everything beautiful came
tumbling out of it, down a long, silken ladder, and it fell all gold
and silver into the sea in a shower like a firework, and when it
fell, I looked up and I could see into heaven. But heaven was
here. It wasn't in the sky. It was between my eyes and the sky, it
was everywhere, we were all part of it. I saw heaven.
Lottie You shouldn't say that, it's wicked to tell lies like that.
Young B But I did see it, I did, I did. I wanted to shout and shout and sing
and dance on the beach, it was so beautiful, and if I had run into
the sea I should have danced on top of the water, everyone would
have seen me and clapped their hands and danced for joy.
Lottie Did you really see it?
Young B Yes, yes.
Lottie Heaven?
Young B Yes.
Lottie Angels?
Young B Look. There are angels in that rock pool. Look. If I put my hands
down and cup them together and bring up the water. I've got a

star fish and a shell and some sand – and hundreds and thousands of angels, tiny ones, like gold pins, look . . .

Lottie You're a liar.

Young B Look.

Lottie You've just got a handful of stupid old water and a bit of mouldy green weed. That's all I can see.

Young B Oh, how can you not see, Lottie, how can you not?

Lottie I'll tell father what you said.

Young B Tell him, tell him. Tell everybody!

Lesage (*Reading*) 'Drosera Rotundiflora is widely spread in bogs. The genus is a large one and found in most parts of the world. The habit, shape and size of the leaves vary. Often there is a creeping rhizome with rosettes of leaves which may have stalks and rounded blades. The blade is covered with small tentacles, which are hair-like growths containing vascular bundles, and ending in swollen reddish heads, which secrete a sticky, glistening fluid. In addition to these stalked glands there are very numerous small sessile glands of a dome shape, of two cells on a short stalk. The excretion on the top of the tentacles is probably mistaken by insects for nectar, with fatal results for those deceived. They remain stuck, they struggle and the tentacles are exceedingly sensitive and bend with an inward and downward movement, the insect being finally placed on the leaf blade. The stimulus passes to surrounding tentacles which bend towards the same spot, entombing and smothering the victim.'

Mrs L What a nasty thing!

Lesage You don't like it?

Mrs L Eating insects. Makes me shudder.

Lesage I mean the style. The writing.

Mrs L Oh, yes. Very nice. You always did know how to write things. Very literary.

Lesage It's a botanical description. It's part of my monograph on the carnivorous plants.

Mrs L I tried to get a chat going with that Mrs Smithers again tonight. Nice sort of person, I thought. She's doing a Queen Anne style armchair in gold velvet. Advanced work, that is. Velvet's tricky. With fringeing, of course. I admired it. Well, that's the way to get to know someone, isn't it? Admiring something they're doing. You've got to make a start. It isn't like it used to be.

During the war you could talk to anyone. We all had something in common, we were all in the same boat then. (*Pause*) It was no use. She wasn't a bit friendly.

Lesage Mrs Smithers?

Mrs L I did try. I like to make new friends. Have a chat. I get lonely. I've always been a sociable person.

Lesage I sat. I made plans. I had ideas. I'm always having them. Every day, up they come like bubbles on a fish tank. Pop-pop. What happens?

Mrs L You should go to him. Go and tell him, if he isn't fit to run the job from the top he should make way for a younger man.

Lesage I've even thought of applying elsewhere.

Mrs L You've worked. You're ambitious. You're entitled to a say-so.

Lesage If we could just co-operate, work as a team. We get on. I've even got admiration for him. Well, I used to. He did some good work. I'd respect for him. If he'd just stop mooning about. That's all . . .

Mrs L Lost his grip.

Lesage He's only 53.

Mrs L I'll make some buttered toast.

Lesage A series of pamphlets, I thought. Soft card covers, an illustration from a Victorian botanical companion. Introductions to the various species. Well, he could do one – write about those lilies he's so fond of. There'd be a series of them, people would collect them. Nothing too expensive, not to cost more than – say, 20 or 25 pence. Written in plain language, but accurate. Scientific but descriptive. Different colour cover for each title – pastels, I thought, fondant colours – pink, blue, pale green, lemon . . .

Mrs L You always had a sweet tooth. Not that you'd too many sweets as a child. Well, you couldn't, with . . .

Lesage The rationing.

Mrs L Yes.

Lesage Toast doesn't taste the same done on a gas-fire. It hasn't got the same . . . smoky flavour.

Mrs L Get a home of your own, a wife to clean the grates out. Then you can have a coal fire.

Lesage I'd like a wife.

Mrs L You won't get modern girls going down on their hands and knees every morning to mucky coals.

Lesage I'm 31.

Mrs L Plenty of time.

Lesage I've a good job . . . if I could just . . .

Mrs L Have it out with him. You won't get anywhere, come grumbling to me. A man has to stand up for himself.

Lesage Maybe he's got – a secret sorrow.

Mrs L A trouble shared is a trouble halved. We found *that* out in 1940.

(*The surgery*)

Bowman I become – anxious. People begin to notice. I am not myself. They see me . . .

Doctor Open wider . . .

(*Bowman gurgles*)

Tongue flat. Good.

Bowman I am quite well. I wondered if . . . my age . . . But I remember when it began, it began when I was born.

Doctor Just the right shirt sleeve, now, up above the elbow.

Bowman You see I should be relieved to have a . . . a natural explanation. Strain, some infection.

Doctor It will feel a little constricted for a second or two.

Bowman I feel . . . foolish.

Doctor Rest your arm on the desk.

Bowman People have seemed – uneasy in my company. Since it began. They know something is – unusual. My assistant – Lesage, looks at me . . . how can I tell anyone? It comes without warning.

Doctor Just relax your leg.

Bowman I am fifty-three. I have a responsible job. I'm very happy. I am writing a book about lilies.

Doctor I should like your shirt off now, please.

Bowman I have the job I dreamed about when I was a boy – a young man. Working among flowers. Trees. When I was a child, I could never stop staring at leaves, petals . . . the vegetable world. It seemed miraculous. It *is* miraculous.

Doctor Deep breath in.

(*He breathes in. Tries to speak*)

Breathe out slowly. That's fine. Shirt back on again.

Bowman I have everything I could want. But there is so much . . . I see so much beauty. I have visions of angels. For a year . . . never since childhood, years of darkness, silence, and then, suddenly . . . I am fifty-three years old.

Doctor Ears? Just keep your head still. Fine.

Bowman I wish you could see what I see. No one could want more. I wish everyone could see. You think I am going mad. You think I'm taking drugs or drinking, or . . .

Doctor No.

Bowman The world is a perfect creation. Everything lives. The timeless present. There is nothing dead, nothing is wasted, nothing is past. Everything shares the same life, everything is here, now. Here *is* now, time and space are synonymous. Everything living is perfect, throbbing with life and meaning and streaming with light. Plants – I see the life flowing in and out of the plants I touch, I can hear them singing. If you cut a plant down it weeps. It bleeds. I can hear the plants weeping. The middle air is filled with angels, there is only this reality – the world is overspilling with love. My gardens are leaping and iridescent with the love of God.

Doctor You are perfectly well.

Bowman Yes.

Doctor I cannot relieve you of your visions. I cannot bear them for you. I cannot absolve you of the responsibility of them. I can give you tablets to thicken your blood, and tablets to make you calm and tablets to send you to sleep. I can staunch the flow from a wound and splint a broken limb, I can eradicate a thousand petty ailments of the flesh, real and imaginary. I cannot relieve you of your visions.

Bowman But you believe me.

Doctor Certainly. But what is it you want of me? A cure? A miracle? I cannot give you either.

Bowman No.

Doctor I cannot help you.

(*Susannah's bedroom*)

Nurse Look now, that cat, on your bed again. What have I said? What has your mother said?

Susannah He's so warm. I like to feel him against me. I like to watch his face when he's asleep. He dreams. What do cats dream about?

Nurse I'm going to run your bath. Nice and warm.

Susannah Perhaps they're nightmares. He twitches all over, his eyes roll and his whiskers flick about. And his paws. As if it were some-thing frightening. Being torn to pieces and gobbled up by ravening wolves.

Nurse He's a kitchen cat. That's where he should be – downstairs.

That's not the place for him, your bed. Cats bring diseases.

Susannah Do cats have souls?

Nurse Fleas.

Susannah Last night, I dreamed I was drowning. I was sinking down and down into green water, bluey-green, and I breathed in the water, it filled my lungs. It tasted *sweet*. I dreamed I would die in the water and that was where heaven was. 'Those are pearls that were his eyes.' I like that. I like to think of my bones being turned into coral and my eyes into pearls.

Nurse You do too much reading.

Susannah You learn everything that way. What's in the world and out of the world.

Nurse We'll have you up.

Susannah I can have dreams whenever I want them. I can dream in the daytime. I don't even have to close my eyes. I can go anywhere. You should see my dreams.

Nurse Time-wasting.

Susannah Why? Why?

Nurse Real things. That's our concern. Real things.

Susannah What are real? Chairs and tables? The sky through the window, grey as an old blanket. Rain dribbling along the gutters.

Nurse It'll brighten up. The forecast said it'd clear.

Susannah What I see is real, what I dream is real. Realer than the things you call real. It doesn't matter if I'm asleep or awake. Like drowning under the sea. That was real. Sometimes I dream I'm climbing a mountain. Or I'm in a jungle. A thick, dark, steamy jungle, where all the leaves are big and flat as plates and dark, dark green, and there are faces peering out of the leaves. There are noises all around. Stamping and snuffling. Animals. I smell them and they smell me and then we know there's no need to fear. I don't. I'm not afraid of anything now.

Nurse There's the embroidery set your mother bought you. There's that to start on.

Susannah And then I can dream when I sew, stitch-stitch, stitch-stitch and if I prick my finger, the blood will run like rain, bright blood. Isn't blood a strange thing? It tastes of metal. I lick my finger and taste my own blood, and that's what it's like inside myself. A thick, slow, dark-red river running between the banks of my veins. Like another sort of jungle.

Nurse You've that friend coming to tea.

Susannah Alice.

Nurse You'll enjoy that.

Susannah Alice doesn't ever dream. Her father's dead. He killed himself. He laid down on the railway line and the red blood ran.

Nurse That's not a thing to talk about. You shouldn't have been told about that.

Susannah Alice told me. I should try and be kind to her. She needs kindness. But I don't like her very much. And all she wants to talk about is horses.

Nurse I had a horse. When I was girl. A pony.

Susannah Did you live in the country?

Nurse It's all built over now. Nothing's the same.

Susannah What a lot of things I don't know about you. I don't even know how old you are.

Nurse Because it isn't any of your business, Miss. Now – out you get. You don't want a cold bath, do you?

(*Bowman's office*)

Bowman I've been looking at the lilies. Standing here. The lilies are very fine. Very fine.

Lesage I was wondering about lunch.

Bowman The trumpet hybrids. Green dragon. African Queen. Look at the beauty of them. I stare and stare at them, I find myself unable to avert my eyes.

Lesage I wanted to – have a chat. Things in general. I thought I could buy you lunch.

Bowman To eat flowers. Think of that. To taste the petals against the tongue. Lilies – camellias. The scent of lilies in the mouth.

Lesage Very nice for the bees. I'm sure.

Bowman You were talking of lunch?

Lesage I thought it would be pleasant. I'd like – I said – a chat. This and the other.

Bowman You always seemed to have – your own friends. Company. I envy you.

Lesage I'd be glad of the chance.

Bowman Oh. Thank you. Yes. Thank you.

(*Fade*)

(*The restaurant*)

Lesage I'd like to think that we could – that you saw me as part of a team. Subordinate, of course. I have my side of things to attend

116

to. You've the overall responsibility. But we seemed – out of touch.

Bowman I give you too much to do? Perhaps . . . is it a question of under-staffing? I had hoped – things always used to run smoothly. I thought they did so.

Lesage I've new ideas, new plans. As I see it, we've a duty to the public. We are a Public Gardens. We should make them an attraction. And we can educate. That was the basis of my idea about the series of pamphlets.

Bowman Pamphlets?

Lesage You didn't hear?

Bowman I . . . Oh, yes. Yes . . .

Lesage And then, of course, we're a scientific institution. There's the botanical research, experimentation. New strains, new develop-ments in soil management and so on.

Bowman You are – a practical man. Yes.

Lesage I like to think so.

Bowman There's so much . . .

Lesage Naturally some things appeal to you more than others. And to me. Naturally. That's why it's a question of collaboration. Delegation but . . .

Bowman We may be understaffed. I've neglected things.

Lesage No, No. We're *over*-staffed. We should be more streamlined. For example, six assistant curators, as follows – Tropical, Arboretum North, Temperate, Arboretum South, herbaceous and decorative. North and South could merge and decorative is superfluous. I've saved you two jobs. Two salaries. We need the money for other developments. Rebuilding. Costs are going up every day.

Bowman I should not want to put men out of work.

Lesage O'Brien retires in eighteen months.

Bowman You seem to – you've made a study of it. You feel I take you too much for granted.

Lesage Would you care for cheese?

Bowman No. I eat frugally in the middle of the day.

Lesage It's your health? I'm sorry to hear you're unwell.

Bowman Not unwell. I was assured of that.

Lesage You felt you should check?

Bowman It is not – an illness.

Lesage Oh. Well – I'm glad to hear that.

Bowman Do I seem unwell to you? The way you look at me, as if I were failing...

Lesage Oh, no, no. Probably tiredness.

Bowman You are a young man.

Lesage Thirty-one.

Bowman You have the world before you. That is how it must seem to you.

Lesage I've chosen my corner of it.

Bowman You're unhappy here? Your work is perhaps unsatisfying. Yes.

Lesage You see – it's a question of what I believe I could do. The opportunities open. What I can see might develop.

Bowman I had no real ambitions. Chances presented themselves unexpectedly, promotion, responsibility – they were unasked for. Undeserved? Perhaps so. Perhaps I lack the proper qualities – the real talents. When I was your age, I was less...

Lesage It isn't a question of ambition for myself. I don't want to seem pushing. It's the job. The future of the work.

Bowman Have you a family?

Lesage I've my mother. Just for the present, I live with my mother.

Bowman I had two sisters and two brothers. We were happy. Close. We shared things. Tumbled about together.

Lesage I'm an only child myself.

Bowman I miss them. I had forgotten how I miss them.

Lesage Dead?

Bowman Two dead. The others – oh, away, married, immersed in their own lives. Grown up. It seems to me that I did not grow up, as they did. And in some way, it doesn't surprise me. I was always – I felt somehow separate. Isolated by things I saw, things I felt. There has always seemed to be a distance.

Lesage You never thought of marriage?

Bowman No. I should not make a wife happy. I should not know how. I'm a solitary man. Certain things – keep me away from others. It isn't what I would have chosen. It isn't ideal. The world is a whole. An entity. All life is one. Do you understand?

Lesage You're lonely.

Bowman Yes. Sometimes that.

Lesage I'll confide to you that I should like a wife. I see myself as a family man.

Bowman There should be no barriers, there *are* no barriers, between any of us. And yet there are. There are.

Lesage I've always been – well, on the shy side I suppose.

Bowman Oh no, not that. More than that. There is a fundamental – I have all the world and yet I have nothing. You don't see.

Lesage Not – exactly.

Bowman No.

Lesage I find there's simply the difficulty of meeting – the right person. One needs things in common, shared interests. That's the hub of it.

Bowman I like my own company. The evenings are . . . there is so much to think over – the things I see – so much to try and understand. There is a pattern to things, just within my grasp and yet – gone.

Lesage Of course, I think a good deal about my work. It's always occupied me. A wife would have to accept that.

Bowman Oh, find a wife, find love, children, find . . .

Lesage It's not so easy. I don't think it's so easy.

Bowman Do I look ill? Do I look older? I see the same face in the mirror. The same eyes. It is the world which is so different now.

Lesage I'd like to walk over to that area beyond the pergola. I'd one or two ideas for it.

Bowman Go around the gardens?

Lesage If you've half an hour, say.

Bowman I have – all time. There is nothing else.

Lesage I drew up a few plans. Tentative suggestions.

Bowman Do you understand? That time is irrelevant. Time comes or goes. Stands still. There is no *time*.

> (*Music* 1)
> (*The harp accompaniment only to the song* 'The Blessed Damozel')
> (*Fade*)
> (*The sound of the sea*)

Lottie There you are. What are you doing sitting in the conservatory? I've been looking for you all over. Everywhere.

Young
Bowman Go away.

Lottie What are you reading?

Young B Something.

Lottie What do you want to be inside for, it's very, very hot. Mother says it's nearly 90 degrees, it's hotter than it has ever been. Even the sea is boiling hot. I'm going to swim in the sea now. Why aren't you coming?

Young B Go away.

    Lottie Are you in trouble?

Young B I'm reading.

    Lottie What have you done this time?

Young B I said . . . something.

    Lottie What? What did you say?

Young B I told him what I saw.

    Lottie What did you see?

Young B Angels dancing on the water. They had silky hair and clothes like candles' flames. They were dancing.

    Lottie You're not to tell any more of those lies. They are lies, you know they are. Father beats you every time, he will always beat you until you learn. It's wicked. It's the work of the devil. I'm going down to swim. What are you going to do? Have they forbidden you ever to swim again?

Young B No. Anyway, I don't care. I can read about plants.

    Lottie I'm running. I'm going to run and run into the sea. Goodbye, goodbye. Now I'm running.

Young B Now it is very hot. I am lying in the grass with my head in the flowers. If I half-close my eyes, the flowers will merge together, the flowers will dance. Poppies. Swaying red skirts of poppies. And blue larkspur. There are thistles growing up against the stone wall. Thistles as high as a man. Silver grey stalks thicker than my hand and spears for leaves. Spears. And huge purple heads. Purple is the colour of mourning and grief. Lottie likes thistles. Lottie plays a game with them, a game of dying. Lottie likes the smell of the salt when it dries on her legs. She licks it. Lottie likes sand and sea. I can see Lottie, by the water. She runs and runs and her hair flies backwards and now she is in the sea, she has dived in where the sun lies in a band across the blue, she is swimming away, swimming away, far out, far out . . .

    (*The 'visionary theme' music appears*)

Young B Oh . . . now she is flying, now she is coming up out of the sea, she is very near to me, I could reach out and touch her, she is not here and she is not there, she is everywhere, she is . . . there are two of them. They are lifting her, carrying her, one of them has hold of her hands, they are dancing. Oh beautiful! How beautiful! Her hair is flying, flying. Oh, goodbye Lottie, goodbye, goodbye, goodbye . . .

(Bowman and Lesage walking round the gardens)

Bowman My sister died.

Lesage And you say you were beaten?

Bowman They thought I was telling lies. They always thought so. Oh, and you think so. You listen with such careful politeness, set your face in that expression of . . .

Lesage Well, I suppose . . . the Bible is full of angels. I had to learn a great deal of the Bible, when I was younger.

Bowman But you don't believe me! No one believes.

Lesage I – I keep an open mind. Things of that sort have never . . . I'm more of a practical man.

Bowman No, no. The minds of all the people are closed. I suppose it is scarcely surprising. I knock upon doors, but no one opens them. People have eyes but they can't see. Listen, I'm telling you that . . . what I am telling you is the truth. There are so few people I have tried to tell. You seem to want – to understand. I've shocked you.

Lesage Perhaps we just live in different worlds. Perhaps it's that. I believe you're . . . honest.

Bowman But deluded.

Lesage I couldn't say . . .

Bowman I *can* say. That I had a vision of my sister Charlotte caught up by angels, led by the hand. There was light streaming down, glittering on the surface of the sea. I felt *happy*. It was the same light we can see now. It's all the same. Do you know the poet William Blake sat up for the whole of one night with his brother who was dying, and towards dawn he saw the spirit leave his body and wing its way to heaven, clapping its hands for joy.

Lesage I've never been much of a religious man.

Bowman No, no! It is *this* world, here and now, everywhere – it is what I see, all around me, all the time . . . reality.

Lesage If we go down the path here, we get a good view of the area from a distance, as it were, perhaps you'll appreciate . . .

Bowman What I have seen I know, I know to be true. My father beat me for lying. And ever since that day, until now, I've seen nothing, there were long, dark years. From the day my sister died until this year, on March 24th, I saw the magnolia tree by the west wall full of angels and blazing with the light of God. I came out of my room and it was there, I *saw* . . . the years between were nothing. I never forgot. But nothing. Until now, this year,

March . . . I see nothing else. I can think of nothing else.

Lesage It's . . . disturbing.

Bowman You think I'm out of my mind.

Lesage It's only that I've no experience, nothing to go on, I wish I could . . . imagine.

Bowman 'Imagination' they said. It was another word for lies. They beat me. They . . . Ah!

Lesage Something's wrong?

Bowman The child . . . the girl. There she is . . . over there. Again.

Lesage The girl in the wheelchair?

Bowman I see her every day now. She comes here every afternoon. She looks . . .

Lesage Very ill. Pale.

Bowman There's something about her face, something I recognise . . . I've wanted to talk to her, you know? Ask her . . .

Lesage Both legs in those iron frames – it's people like that we cater for. They get pleasure, coming here, seeing the gardens.

Bowman I . . . I should speak to her . . .

Lesage She's going the other way. If you'd care to give me your opinion, now, about these few plans . . .

(*The psychiatrist's room*)

Bowman It seems I have to go on searching. I need – something. Advice. Help. Understanding. Yes. If I could make someone else understand.

Doctor You are . . . yes . . . fifty-three.

Bowman I was born in the country. Kent, in a house with wide windows and a nest of martins in the eaves and bees booming in the garden. I was born in a room overlooking the tumbling wisteria and honeysuckle, and the pale pink rose Albertine grew over the wall. My father grew lilies. Great, white virginal lilies with spotted tongues, and tiger lilies, and lilies the colour of a dragon's back. Oh, the smell of them, that sweet, sinister smell. Panther lilies with orange recurving flowers.

Doctor What about your family?

Bowman Two brothers. One dead in 1940. Two sisters, one drowned. I saw her drowned and carried away by angels.

Doctor Married? Children?

Bowman No, no. I never wanted them. I never wanted other people.

Until now. Now, I feel the need – but would a family understand?

Doctor Tell me your visions.

Bowman Tell . . how? How can I? No one else sees. I tried to talk to Lesage. Lesage would catalogue them and file the details under A-Z, he would measure them and weigh them. But I didn't seem able to – explain to him. The words are always wrong.

Doctor Are you worried by this – Lesage?

Bowman Worried? No. No. He wants to have my job. Perhaps others do. Perhaps I should give it to them. I am – I fear I've become incompetent. Absorbed. My head sings. The last few months have been . . . I no longer seem able to concentrate. You see, what I see, what I know becomes the only reality. This – the chair, the table, the book, the desk . . . none of it counts. It is real and yet insubstantial.

Doctor Does this other reality stay with you? Does it vanish?

Bowman It's absorbed – transformed . . . light pours down upon it, everything is caught up in it – this beauty, this . . . love. It is love. Words make it a nonsense. It won't be trapped in words. It began when I was born. The new creation. I hear music – singing. A very high, silvery sound. The light is the music and the music is the light. Eyes and ears are one. It is all soaked up through every pore of my skin. I do not simply see, simply hear. Those are the limitations of the flesh. The visions are . . .

Doctor Spirit?

Bowman Yes. But flesh, too. Everything is – one. Angels dancing, going up and down a ladder to heaven. And rainbows, and the water is like mercury, silver, pure, transparent. I hold my hands under the water and it streams over them like light, my hands are bathed iin it. And the taste of everything is sweeter. There is a sweetness n the flesh.

    (*Pause*)

If I turn my head, I will know how you are looking at me. I know without turning my head.

Doctor I could send you away. Rest. Mountains. Isolation. A holiday.

Bowman Yes.

Doctor I could prescribe – small blue tablets or large white tablets. I could send you to a priest.

Bowman But you do not understand and you cannot help me.

Doctor We could delve into your childhood. We could forage in the soil of your mind and bring up roots, stones, the skeletons of old, buried leaves.

Bowman It would be no use.

Doctor No. No use.

Bowman What should I do? Am I mad?

Doctor What is madness?

Bowman Am I fit to work? Should I simply give up, retire . . .

Doctor Only you can say.

Bowman I need just one more person to accept what I see. All life is eternal and the same, all things work for each other's good and love is the foundation of the world.

Doctor Have you considered – you are a very fortunate man.

Bowman I would give anything for it to be taken away. For ordinary life. Work. Why should I see what I see? I'm a – dull man.

Doctor Others would envy you.

Bowman No one would.

Doctor Perhaps . . . I envy you. Yes. I envy you.

(*Susannah in bed*)

Susannah Tom. Tom. Puss. Here. Come here. On the bed. It's all right, she's not here, she's gone downstairs. I shouldn't be awake. There – good cat. You're very warm. You purr so loudly. It was cold in the garden. We went all the way round and then she sat on a bench for a bit. We watched people going by. It's funny how they look at me. Or don't look. Sometimes they stare and stare. Sometimes they lower their heads and walk by very quickly and I can see what they're thinking. Wondering. I suppose I embarrass them. They wouldn't know what to say. Sometimes they do smile. But most of the people don't smile at anything. How stiff their faces are. Grey and stiff, as if they were only half-alive. All the cares of the world. They don't look around them. The fountains shoot up like silver from the middle of the lake, and there are so many different flowers. So many colours. And they still don't look. I suppose they have troubles. Unhappy faces. I should like to change them. I should like all the faces to laugh. Last night I dreamed I was in a huge library full of great, heavy books with leather bindings. Dull books. Brown and black books. But when I looked at them I saw they'd all got faces too, and they weren't miserable. All the books on the shelves were laughing and laughing. If I tickle you under the chin you yawn and that looks like a laugh. You're like the Cheshire cat. And you haven't got germs or fleas, and anyway, I think I like fleas. Little jumping things. Jump-jump-jump. What a way to get about. I wish I could jump. I'd do it everywhere. The cages on my legs would clank and then everybody would laugh. If I close my eyes, I can see them. I can see them all – all laughing.

Lesage Well, I did try. Nobody can say I didn't try. We ate a good lunch. Roast beef and rhubarb pie. He wouldn't have cheese. The waitress was nice, as well. Trim.

Mrs L What's the time now?

Lesage What do you keep asking me the time for, every five minutes?

Mrs L You're as bad as he is, strikes me. You don't listen either. Full of your own talk. No wonder I look for company.

Lesage Oh – Mrs Smithers. Yes.

Mrs L I've laid the coffee tray out with a cloth. Everything nice. And a plate of home-made biscuits. Spice biscuits.

Lesage I'll type those notes out, and leave them on his desk. I explained it all to him, what I had in mind. Not that he'll read them. He said the magnolia tree was full of angels. Light, he said, light streaming down. It was like a bonfire, he said, like the burning bush.

Mrs L That's how it takes some. It's a mania. Like an illness. Religious mania.

Lesage No – no, I don't think it is. He seems – it changes him. I looked at his face. His face was full of it. Full of something. He goes about looking half-asleep. His eyes are dead, dull. He seems to be miles off. But it changed. I couldn't follow.

Mrs L I said eight o'clock. Any time around eight.

Lesage I told him everything. Talked. He didn't seem to listen. It was as though he was paying attention and couldn't, as if there was something more important.

Mrs L A friend of your father's got religious mania. He'd had shell shock, oh, back in 1916 in the trenches. His head buzzed. They couldn't do anything. And then, when it all started up again, all those air-raids, it turned him. He went around carrying a banner and giving out leaflets. 'Praise ye the Lord for the avenging of Israel, when the people willingly offered themselves.' He'd walk about the streets night after night. It didn't seem to bother him, the danger. And he never wore a coat. Never seemed to lose his way, and there was blackout all round. Harmless, I suppose. They tried to get him work. Fire watching. He'd done well in 1916, so they said.

'The bows of the fighting men are broken and they that stumbled are girded with strength'. Funny, how I remember a lot of what he said. He had it all in his poor head.

Lesage Mrs Smithers is late.

Mrs L She'll come.

Lesage I don't think he understands how frustrating it is. My hands are tied. What can I do? I'd like to understand him. Help him. I don't see how. He's been to doctors.

Mrs L Delusion. Just like him – Percy Ormerod, that was it. He lasted, though. You'd have thought he'd get a direct hit, buried under falling rubble, anything like that. Anything could have happened. It never did. Where are you going?

Lesage I might as well carry on. Perhaps if I finish one of the pamphlets, about the carnivorous plants, he'll take more interest. They'd sell. It's something I'd take a pride in. It's an outlet. Then he could follow it up with one about lilies. There's nothing he doesn't know about lilies. If he'd just concentrate – get it all down. People are interested. Keen. I don't think he knows.

Mrs L I want you down here. I want you to meet Mrs Smithers.

Lesage She's not coming is she?

Mrs L She's got delayed.

Lesage You said yourself she wasn't friendly. Didn't want to chat. Not really.

Mrs L She's a widow. She lives alone.

Lesage Keeps herself to herself. By the look of things.

Mrs L You've got to make an effort. Draw people out. They're always grateful.

Lesage That's what I tried. Only – it was as though he couldn't put it all into words. Not sensible words. I wish I could have followed him, a bit more. We're different.

Mrs L I told her all about you. Mrs Smithers. She's got no family. She seemed interested.

Lesage People mind their own business.

Mrs L They never used to. Share and share alike. Well, human beings were made for it. They never used to be so shut up inside themselves.

Susannah I like to look at the people.

Nurse I thought it was the plants you were so keen on. All those names you've got off by heart.

Susannah If there were no flowers at all, no trees and no grass, nothing, if everything was grey and black and dead, if there wasn't any water or sunlight, do you suppose they'd notice? They all go by with bent heads. They frown. And I see it all. What will it be like when I don't have to look only through my eyes? Eyes are such a hindrance. Don't you feel that? Like these awful iron legs. I can't jump. I can't run, I feel very tired of living.

Nurse That's a wicked thing to say.

Susannah Flesh and blood and bones are so heavy. Like a plaster cast. Like these irons. They drag me down. I'd like to fly and fly.

(*Music*)
(*Plant Chorus*)

Chorus one	*Chorus two*
Berberis	Lavender
Cypress	Calendula
Larkspur	Petunia
Cornflower	Nemetia
Salvia	Zinnia
Columbine	Veronica
Aquilegea	Potentilla
Japonica	Tamarix
Crocus	Thyme

(*Susannah's own voice comes out of them, half-speaking, half-chanting*)

Susannah Redbird. Garnet. Apollo. Leonie. Swan Lake. Excelsior. Green Goddess. Journey's End.

Bowman You know all my lilies.

Susannah I learned them.

Bowman I often see you.

Susannah Every day. I see you too. Why are they your lilies?

Bowman I had them planted. I look out of my office window at them.

Susannah Do you work here? You can't be a gardener because you don't wear a brown coat.

Bowman No, I . . . Oh, look! Look!

Susannah Where?

Bowman At the tree. The magnolia tree.

(*The 'visionary music' begins to ripple out*)

Bowman I hear the music. Listen. It's coming from the tree. I see the bees dancing. The bees are gold and silver. The leaves are shimmering. Don't you see?

Susannah No. But I believe you do. Your eyes are open. Everyone else's are closed. They bow their heads and look at the ground. They have so many troubles.

Bowman I try to tell them.

Susannah But they wouldn't understand.

Bowman Do you?

Susannah Oh yes. All I can see are – flowers – colours – the grass – the fountains. But I know what you see. I can tell by looking at your face. Every time I come here I see something new. Different. I think it's because I look so hard. And because I'm dying. But the bees look like ordinary bees.

Bowman It's fading. It always fades. It doesn't last.

Susannah But it will come back won't it? You know that.

Bowman Yes.

Susannah So it's all right. You just have to wait until it does. And not look at the ground. Here's my nurse coming back.

Nurse Now Susannah . . .

Susannah This is a friend of mine. Don't you recognise him? We see him nearly every day. He owns all the lilies.

Bowman Bowman. Charles Bowman.

Nurse Owns the lilies?

Bowman Curator. I . . .

Susannah Keeper of the lilies. A lily-white boy. Will you push my chair?

Nurse Susannah . . .

Bowman I'll push you, yes.

Susannah Around the whole gardens?

Bowman Anywhere at all.

Susannah We may see anything. Oh, anything!

(*The plant music without chorus. It fades*)

Susannah Ground elder. Bishop's weed. Fool's parsley. Sweet Cicely. Corn Caraway. Wild Angelica. Shepherd's needle. Honesty.

Bowman Lunaria Annua. That's honesty.

Susannah Lunaria Annua. Yes. That's right, isn't it? They do look like that. Little silky moons.

Bowman Where do you live, Susannah?

Susannah In a tall, tall house with a lion for a doorknocker and windows curtained against the sun and the tops of sycamore trees waving in front of my window. You could come and see me there. Will you come?

Bowman If you'd like it . . . I rarely go out.

Susannah You must come. Haven't you many friends?

Bowman No . . . no, not many. I'm very glad I met you.

Susannah My nurse gets bored. 'All those trees,' she says. 'All those trees.' I suppose it's tiring for her, pushing me everywhere. She likes a 'nice sit-down.' I look at the trees.

Bowman 'The tree which moves some to tears of joy is, in the eyes of others, only a green thing which stands in the way.'

Susannah But I'm lucky. I haven't any troubles. They don't know when I'll die , . . . I'd like to wait until the winter. Everything else will die then. But people look after me. I have every day to look at things. Everyone else has to work and worry. I learned something, too. I read a lot of books. I can always read.

Bowman What did you learn?

Susannah 'The stars reflect the visions of holiness and the trees are uttering prophecies and speaking instructive words to the sons of men.'

Bowman That's the truth. That's what I see. Oh, Susannah, don't die. You mustn't die.

Susannah I shall. I don't seem to belong here now. It's a nuisance. I feel like a shot bird. Heavy.

Bowman We've reached the edge of the lake.

Susannah 'Every night and every morn
Some to misery are born.
Every morn and every night
Some are born to sweet delight.'

What tree is that?

Bowman A tree of heaven.

Susannah What are you looking at now?

Bowman The lake. Look at the lake!

(*The visionary music*)

Listen. Can't you hear it?

Susannah You can.

Bowman 'Let the priests of the raven of dawn no longer in deadly black with hoarse note curse the sons of joy, for everything that lives is holy.'

Susannah I'm glad you came with me. I'm glad it happens to you. Then nothing else will matter. Look – leaves and petals. Water. Bees' wings. Dragonflies.

Bowman But the music has stopped.

Susannah Then now the silence is singing. And the water and the grass.

Bowman Do you see?

Susannah Nothing with my eyes, but everything is in my head. Look at the wind rippling the water.

Bowman It's colder. I should take you back.

Susannah There she sits, black as a crow on her bench.

Bowman She disapproves.

Susannah She doesn't see, that's all. But I like her. It isn't her fault. Turn me round.

Bowman Will you come tomorrow?

Susannah Oh yes! And you'll come to see me and I'll tell you the beautiful names of . . . oh, the butterflies. I know a lot about them, too. Oh. It's half past four. Now, today is almost over. It is the end of this day.

(*Bowman's office*)

Bowman I have thought a great deal about what I should say to you. I lay awake last night. I was so anxious to put things right. But there's nothing I can do. I feel at fault. And yet I'm innocent. You've been unhappy, dissatisfied. How many others. I'm sorry.

Lesage You're thinking of going somewhere else? Making a fresh start.

Bowman No, no. I shall retire. I'm not poor. I'll buy a small house in the country. Dig my garden.

Lesage Grow lilies.

Bowman Oh yes – very many lilies.

Lesage I'm sorry we couldn't see eye to eye – work together.

Bowman You've tried. I see that.

Lesage It's just been difficult – going ahead alone. I've been . . .

Bowman Frustrated.

Lesage In the dark. I had all my plans.

Bowman And now you can have your head.

Lesage They may choose someone else. Somebody older.

Bowman I'll recommend you. I'll write a strong recommendation. It's
what you want, isn't it?

Lesage I hope I've respected your ways of working.

Bowman You've ambitions, ideas. Everything that's needed. Everything
I no longer have. I no longer really care, you see.

Lesage But you'll miss it all. The gardens. The people . . . you'll be very
cut off, in the country by yourself. It's not what you've been
used to.

Bowman It's necessary. It's all I can do.

Lesage Perhaps if you took a holiday – a year off, say. I could take
charge, then . . . things might improve. Settle down again.

Bowman Nothing could change.

Lesage People like you – they have respect.

Bowman No. Not now. Not any longer.

Lesage I might find it too much for me. Too much responsibility. I feel
inadequate.

Bowman Marry. Find love, support. You need it. Don't let yourself be
alone.

Lesage I don't seem to have . . . I don't know how to go about it. I find
it difficult. Something goes wrong. It's like – well, talking to
strangers. I haven't got the knack.

Bowman Well, I'll think about you here. But I shan't envy you. I'm glad
to be going. I look round this office, I look out of my window at
the conservatories and the people wandering up and down the
paths, the gardeners with spades and barrows and earth stains on
the palms of their hands . . . everything I used to be concerned
with. And I no longer care. My own garden will be real to me.
The lilies I plant. The soil, crumbling under my feet, the smells.
That's what I want. To be alone. And to wait, and see . . .
whatever I may see. There's been so little time. I've dreaded
sleep, a great bite, torn out of the day, all the sights and sounds
and music swallowed up in darkness.

Lesage You shouldn't be going.

Bowman I have to.

Lesage I don't have your way of looking at things. I'm more of a down-
to-earth man, I suppose. Ordinary.

Bowman But I've envied you, Lesage.

Lesage You?

Bowman   I've envied almost everyone in the world.

(*Susannah's bedroom*)

Susannah   Read more. Read me some more.

Bowman   You're tired.

Susannah   I feel pinned down under blocks of stone. Nothing flies any more. Nothing sings.

Bowman   'I see a lily on thy brow,
With anguish moist and fever dew.'

Susannah   My name means 'a lily'.

Bowman   I'll bring you some more tomorrow. I'll cut them freshly.

Susannah   When you cut lilies, they weep.

Bowman   Tomorrow, I'll come earlier. Very early.

Susannah   Tell me what you see now.

Bowman   A girl. White flowers. Lilium candidum. Dark hair on a white pillow.

Susannah   And what do you hear?

Bowman   Silence. Only silence.

Susannah   I wish I could come with you to the gardens. I shall never see them again.

Bowman   You will. You *must*.

Susannah   No. But think of what you may see. The world in a grain of sand or . . . right into the heart of heaven. You may see anything.

Bowman   I shan't be there for much longer. At the gardens.

Susannah   You're going away?

Bowman   Soon. I've bought a house and a garden. I'll write my book about lilies. I'll grow hundreds of things . . . lilies, roses, bushes of lavender, damson trees, quince trees, beds of rosemary and thyme . . .

Susannah   Then someone else will own the lilies.

Bowman   Yes. And the tree of heaven and the dog violets and the milky moon flowers.

Susannah   You must tell your visions. Some people pick flowers and press them between the pages of heavy books and all the colour fades away.

Bowman   But that's not how it will be. I shall keep a hive of bees.

Susannah   *You must tell your visions.* If you press them and keep them, they'll suffocate and die. You can only keep by giving away.

Bowman   When you go, I shall have no one. Nothing.

Susannah   You'll have everything. You will have the world.

132

(Bowman reads the following passage over quietly. Towards the end, the visionary music creeps in)

Bowman 'The madonna lily, lilium candidum, was grown in Roman gardens, mentioned by Greek poets, used in Assyrian sculptures and earlier still, found in Egyptian tombs and featured in designs for floor and wall decorations and vases, in the palace of Knossos in Ancient Crete. The name Madonna Lily originated in the 19th century. Before that, lilium candidum was known simply as the white lily. It is also known as the Bourbon lily and St Joseph's lily. It was grown as a medicinal plant in the monastery gardens of medieval England . . . '
What is it? Something happened? What's happened?

(The music stops. Silence)
Susannah. Susannah is dead. At that moment . . . I knew. I knew when it happened. I have . . . the secret. Life and death. The clear truth. All things . . . fire and water, air and angels, the whole of time gathered together into the moment. Time stops. It is . . . it is love. I have known *love*.
(Fade)

(The sound of digging in soil. The soil being turned over. The visionary music)

Bowman What is it? Susannah? Susannah. There you are. There. Somewhere. If I put out my hand, I should . . . No. There's nothing to see. But everything is here. There are – the white lily petals. A tree. Bees. A yellow butterfly. The sun is shining. Nothing else. But the blind see and the dumb speak and the lame walk. It may never come back but that doesn't matter now *(Softly)* Susannah. Well . . . I have to cultivate my garden.
(Sound of digging again)
(Fade)
(Susannah's voice. Very faintly. The high, wordless singing of the chorus comes in, and takes over on its own at the end)

Susannah 'The corn was orient and immortal wheat, which never should be reaped nor was ever sown. I thought it had stood from everlasting to everlasting. The dust and stones of the street were as precious as gold. The green trees when I saw them first transported and ravished me, their sweetness and beauty made my heart leap, they were such strange and wonderful things. And young men glittering and sparkling, angels and maids strange seraphic pieces of life and beauty. Boys and girls tumbling in the street and playing, were like moving jewels. I knew not that they were born or should die. Eternity was manifest in the light of the day, and something infinite behind everything appeared, which tailed with my expectation and moved my desire. The city seemed to stand in Eden or to be built in heaven. The streets were mine, the temple was mine, the people were mine, their clothes and gold and silver was mine, as much as their sparkling eyes, fair skins and ruddy faces. The skies were mine and so were the sun and moon and stars, all the world was mine, and I the only spectator and enjoyer of it.'

Strip Jack Naked

Strip Jack Naked was first broadcast on BBC Radio 3, on 1 December 1974, with the following cast.

JAMES	*Ian Richardson*
RANDAL	*Dinsdale Landen*
DIANA	*Sian Phillips*

Produced by Richard Wortley.

(James's room. Fade up, austere modern music for string quartet. Pause. It ends. James clicks off the radio. Sighs. Propels his wheelchair across the room towards the window)

James Grey, grey and grey. Why does the sun never shine now? That first summer here, it shone and shone, and the nights were always clear. The moon rode, over the barrow.

    (Pause)

Oh, where's my bloody breakfast? *(Shouts)* Randal?

RANDAL?

He won't come. It hasn't struck eight o'clock yet and he comes on the dot of eight. Which is what I chose, after all, a new life, meticulously ordered. *(Pause)*

Shine, damn you, sun! And I am *hungry.*

If I were master and Randal a servant, I could shout and he would have to come. If wishes were horses, beggars might ride.

Diana used to shout to Mrs Moon, and she always came . . . running. Funny little woman. Like a weasel. When Diana shouted, she . . . but that was because Mrs Moon was rather deaf. *(Pause)*

Oh, I should live alone. And learn to do without the sun.

    (A clock chimes eight. Pause. Door opens. Randal comes in. Carries the breakfast tray down the room. Sets it on the table)

Randal Good morning.

James I said, I should live alone. *(Pause. Randal lays the table)*

And I can do without the sun, mark you. I shall live an entirely grey life.

Randal Oh, the long-range forecast was reasonable.

James For God's sake!

    (He wheels down the room)

And my wheelchair needs mending, you'd better look at it.

Randal What's wrong with it?

James It squeaks, can't you hear? Cloth ears. *(Pause)* No letters? No, Randal, do not tell me, as usual, that there are no letters because I do not write any myself, and that the decision to break with my old acquaintances – you see, I don't pretend to have had *friends* – was entirely mine. It is just that, sometimes, you see, I do miss letters. I suppose I'm allowed that? I daresay Trappist monks occasionally miss the joys of conversation. Do they have to confess to that, I wonder? Well, I have confessed. 'I sometimes miss letters. Forgive me, Randal, for I have sinned.'

(*Pause. He starts to eat*)

Pour yourself some coffee. Why not?

Randal   (*Surprised*) You know I've had mine.

James   Well have some more, fetch yourself a cup. It's all right, I simply feel a little sociable this morning. Eccentric, I know, out of character, I know. But there it is.

Randal   I really don't want any more coffee.

James   Then just sit down. Watch the lions feed. (*Randal sits*) That's right. But don't light a cigarette.

Randal   Have you ever seen me do that, in here?

James   No, no, you're very good. You indulge me.

(*Silence*)

Randal   Isn't it cooked properly?

James   I miss nothing else. I have all I want. Too much, even. Only the letters. (*Pause*)

We used to lie in bed, Diana and I, and wait for them to flop down on to the mat . . . and that was the signal to get up. He was a very punctual postman. I liked that, though I hated anything else in the old life to be punctual or predictable, didn't I?

On Mondays, Wednesdays and Fridays, *she* got up first and made the coffee. On Tuesdays, Thursdays, and Saturdays, I did so. Sundays, we slept late and then quarrelled. Always. Except that, in the end, we didn't even bother to do that.

And what a hell of a lot we used to drink, in those days. I was thinking about that last night. So did you, when you came to see us, so did you. O, don't look so damned polite! Go away, Randal. (*Pause*) Or don't go away, as you please. You're the boss. I suppose. Do you know, I used to bang the top of my egg with a spoon and pick off the bits . . . messy. Like everything else I did then. Not now. Now . . . a neat, clean slice.

(*Pause. He pours coffee*)

Randal   (*Quietly*) James . . . it is Thursday.

(*Long pause. Then James sets down the coffee pot. Picks up the newspaper. Begins to ruffle through it, more and more loudly. Getting slightly hysterical as he reads on*)

James   Text for today. 'The souls of the righteous are in the hand of God, and there shall no torment touch them.' Solomon 3.1. Do you suppose they have a rota of eminent clergymen, or is it picked at random by some sub-editor with a Bible and a pin?

Randal I'm sorry. But you seemed so . . . I though you might have forgotten.

James 'Thomson. To Denise, née Nettlefold, and Roger Thomson, a son (James).'
Wingfield. To Anthea, wife of Captain Dudley Wingfield, a son (James).
Really, I shall have to think of using my middle name in future. James is becoming altogether too common.

Randal You did forget . . . once. You realised when you saw me with my coat on, ready to leave, and . . . it was a shock, then. It was worse.

James 'Boycott, 73. Illingworth l.b.w. for 7. Rain stopped play.'

Randal I've said I'm sorry. I *am*.

James 'Her Royal Highness unveiled a commemorative plaque, toured the Centre and was later entertained to a Civic luncheon at the Town Hall.'

Randal James . . . I have to go, you know that. I always go. Today. Thursday.

(James hurls the newspaper across the room)

James Will you shut up, shut up, shut *up*! It is Thursday, you've told me. Gone on and on reminding me, because once, just once, in three years, I forgot. Do you seriously think I have ever forgotten since? That I don't go to bed on Wednesday nights and lie awake here, alone, shaking . . . with the word Thursday, Thursday, hammering in my head? I dream of the word, Thursday, in neon lights, swaying before my eyes. Choruses of voices, like spectres and furies chant it to me, Randal. I wake before dawn, sick in my guts, knowing that it is Thursday. Sweating. I dread the sound of your steps outside this door. I dread your coming in here, helping me out of bed . . . get washed, dressed and into this chair. Because it is Thursday. I try not to look at your face, because I know where you will be going, and you know, and you still move about in the same measured, relentless way, and look so bloody *calm*. And then you remind me, when you so efficiently and punctually bring in my breakfast, you *remind* me that it is Thursday.

Randal *(Upset)* I've said I'm sorry.

James I heard you.

Randal It won't happen again. (*James laughs*) It's only that I didn't think you minded so much. Not now . . . all this time . . .

James (*Mocking*) 'You didn't think I cared?' Randal, it is because I do not care, or want to care, that I mind so much . . . because I feel guilty . . . *am* guilty. I am to blame because I have never truly cared for years about anything at all. Except myself.

Randal No, you're not to . . .

James Don't you dare tell me I am not to blame. Don't start passing judgement and handing out mercy, Randal. I know the truth about it all . . . past and present. About Diana, about myself. I *know*.

(*Silence. Randal gets up and walks to the table*)

Randal You won't want your breakfast now.

James No. (*Pause*) Randal, I'm . . . thank you, I suppose I mean. Something like that.

Randal All right. Have a rest.

James No. Randal . . . stay. Please.

(*Pause. Randal picks up and folds the newspaper*)

What's it doing outside?

Randal (*At the window*) Grey. There's some mist. You can't see beyond the barrow.

James Rain?

Randal Drizzle.

James Oh, there was always *sun*!

Randal It might brighten up.

James It never 'brightens up.' (*Thoughtful*) The hawk, hovering over the barrow . . .

Randal I haven't seen it lately.

James How boring the birds were in London. When I noticed them at all, in that mad, glittering world of . . . nothing. Grey pigeons, sooty sparrows, dun ducks in the park. Randal . . . you won't tell her . . . what I said about Thursdays?

Randal No.

James It wouldn't interest her. Nothing about me would interest her. Have you described it? This house? this room of mine . . . the barrow out there? The way I live? How different it all is . . . I am. But perhaps she's forgotten who I am.

Randal No.

James She should. I wish *I* were mad and locked away, Randal, then I could forget, too – easily.

Randal She hasn't forgotten. And it's not as you think. She isn't locked away – there are no locks. She could leave.

James Does she ever talk about me? Oh, most of the time, I don't want to hear anything about it at all . . . But other times . . . Does she talk about the child?

Randal She . . . sometimes.

James In distress?

Randal It's . . . hard to say.

James Diana had beautiful hair. I loved that. Even when I had come to hate everything else. It might not have been part of her. Perhaps she talks to them about it . . .

Randal Perhaps.

James I should talk about it . . . about the child, too . . . that water. In distress . . . distress I never felt. How little I have ever felt anything!

Randal Blame, blame, blame!

James Blame. I wallow in it, don't I? (*Pause*) I ought to go there with you. (*Randal sighs*) Oh, not for her sake, she doesn't want to see me. Why should she? No, for my own sake. It might ease the guilt. Bring about a change.

Randal It wouldn't.

James Would it upset her?

Randal It's irrelevant. You won't go.

James *Would* it?

Randal It might, but there's . . .

James Yes?

Randal No. Nothing.

James (*Dangerous*) *Tell* me.

Randal Just that . . . things have changed. She seems a little better.

James 'Seems a little better!'

Randal And they think so, too. The last few weeks . . . months, even, since the spring. I've noticed it.

James She will never be better. She isn't a premature-born child, fighting for its life in an incubator, Randal. Diana – my wife, Diana – your sister, is *mad*.

Randal No! Not in the way you like to think of it.

James *She can never get better.*

Randal You don't *want* her to get better. So long as she is there, shut away, 'Mad', you can feel safe and secure. You can contemplate your navel, indulge yourself. So long as you are here, living this so-called 'new life' . . . Oh, it's all very easy, isn't it? Neat lines, routine, no intrusions or responsibilities. I fetch and carry for you. It's like being in the womb, or the cradle. Why don't you have me take you over completely, think your thoughts for you? You've opted out of life, so you suppose. But that is never possible, and life is not as you choose to see it.

Life is disorganised and messy – even here. Outside the door of this room. There are loose ends, questions, various answers and sometimes . . . no answers. A series of choices, awkward events requiring explanations, accidents. Distress. What Diana is trying to learn to cope with again. But not you. You don't want to take the risk and you don't want Diana to be able to take the risk. You want her to suffer out of sight, while you . . . *wallow*.

James Thank you, Randal, for your sermon on Life. (*Pause*) I could tell you to get out of here and never come back.

Randal And I could tell you . . . 'Take up thy bed and *walk*.'

(*Long silence*)

I'm sorry.

(*Silence*)

I think it's stopped raining.

James You said she was 'a little better'. Since the spring, you said. Why didn't you tell me before? Does it no longer concern me? I'm not a child, Randal, I don't have to have nasty things kept from me.

Randal Nasty things?

James No. (*Pause*) So . . . she may be better. Some day, she may be out of there. Why should that change anything? The damage was done a long time before all that. The damage was done from the start.

Randal I shouldn't have said it. Nothing's certain, not in there. It's all unpredictable. Today I may find her as bad as ever. How do I know? When I go there, when I get out of the car, walk across that gravelled drive, between those right-little, tight-little flowerbeds, *I* feel sick in my guts, *I* want to run away, because it is Thursday, and I do not know what I shall find. She may refuse to look at me, or speak. She's done that sometimes – for two hours. She may not know me – or pretend not to. Or she may talk, spew out a great, messy, incoherent stream of wild talk, her eyes flickering about . . . you . . . me . . . our childhood . . . music you used to play, that six inches of water into which the child fell, the day *I* fell into a cow-pat . . . she confuses us sometimes, did I tell you that? Then there was the filthy meal they had last night, how afraid she is still, things that you and she said to each other. Did. Or else only a dull, dull story about how they all think that the occupational therapist who teaches them pottery had a tiff with her fiancé last Saturday night. Ward gossip. A closed world, obsessed with its own little events. She may weep. She may do nothing but weep. Talk about coming out, home. She may look young and beautiful. She is still beautiful sometimes.

James Oh yes, Diana is beautiful. There are some truths you can never get away from. And her hair.

Randal Oh, anything! (*Pause*) Yes, I might feel better if the sun would shine.

James Do you love your sister? How odd, that I've never really known! I don't mean dutiful, brotherly affection, I mean . . .

Randal Yes. I love my sister.

James Then she has . . . something. You don't love *me*. (*Silence*) You don't even like me now, do you? (*Silence*) But Diana . . .

Randal Would you like some fresh coffee? I think I would.

James Have you ever wanted to kill me?

Randal (*Lightly*) Oh, on some hot, humid afternoon, when you have made me push you to the top of that bloody barrow, I've been tempted to let your wheelchair go.

James Wheeee! I should have a glorious ride, flying through the air. Like the hawk. Did you ever go downhill on a bicycle, with your feet on the handlebars?

Randal Often. Until I came to grief at a left-hand bend and knocked out my front teeth. I was ten.

James I wanted to kill you when you said, 'It is Thursday.'

Randal I know.

James Anyone who has ever lived with one other person, in such confined circumstances, has wanted to kill them. I'm amazed at the restraint of the human race. I believe distracted mothers of small children have homicidal impulses several times a day. It's normal. But that wasn't the case with us, was it? It was an accident . . . surely? Six inches of water. Diana was always so careful.

Randal I know.

James Diana wanted to kill me.

Randal But tried to kill herself instead.

James Courageous. I have no courage. You have. You are a very steady man, Randal, controlled. On the whole.

Randal Some would say 'dull'.

James Oh, I used to, in the old days. 'Spoilsport Randal', I said. 'Dull stick.' In the days when you tried to save me from my worst excesses . . . that hysterical, false life.

Randal You deceive yourself about the old life . . . you enjoyed it.

James The man I was then thought that he did. Not the real man I am now.

Randal You are still you.

James Things change.

Randal Not essentially.

James Here, I feel – reborn.

Randal But you are not.

James What do you know of me? You know *nothing*.

Randal I shall make some fresh coffee. (*Going out*)

James (*Calling*) And a toasted tea-cake?

Randal (*Forgetting. Casual*) No, the baker doesn't call on Thursday. (*Dead silence*)

James And – it – is – Thursday.

(*James's Room. Later*)

Randal (*From the window*) Well, if it was a buzzard, it's gone now.

James (*Absently. Doing a cross-word*) Forget it.

Randal Did you know that they were protected birds?

James Learn something every day.

Randal No, nor did I. Sawyer told me.

James Sawyer of the solitary tooth.

Randal (*Imitating country accent*) ' 'At's a buzzard, 'at is, and you can't go shooting buzzards, you can't, 'ats against the law, see? Protected birds, see?'

James I don't know how you do it. Give you a group of locals and you just melt into them, never discriminate. I couldn't.

Randal It makes a change of scene.

James I shall never need a change of scene.

Randal Early training, maybe. 'Be polite to the villagers. All men are brothers.' So long as you don't pick up their slang and their nasty habits. (*Pause*) No, it's definitely not there now . . . if it was a buzzard.

James It's really not important.

144

Randal Might have been a trick of light, something to do with the mist.

James I only mentioned it for . . . something to say.

Randal It always seems to drag, this last half-hour or so. I never seem to be able to settle to anything.

James Try a cross-word. Take up Yoga.

Randal If I washed up, I'd only break something.

James I do not like *broken* things.

Randal Like that hawk . . . I . . . hover.

James I never used to have time to do cross-words – anyway, I thought them pointless – all games. Actually, there is a good deal of point. Conciseness, filling in a picture-outline, keeping carefully within the frame, neat, block capitals, no untidiness. Satisfying, ultimately.

Randal The mist's dropped down again.

James (*An edge*) Drive carefully!

Randal I must get some more cider from Sawyer.

James Illicit.

Randal Potent.

James Unhygienic – great open barrels. Anything might drop in and decompose.

Randal Oh, it does, so they say – bats drop down, rats climb up and topple in, spiders . . . it's all one in the end, adds to the flavour.

James Do you mind?

Randal Well, the skeletons fall to the bottom, don't they?

James The bottom of that barrow is lined with prehistoric skeletons – their vapours rise.

    (*Randal walks down the room to James*)

Randal I'd better be going. Food all right for you?

James I never have cause for complaint.

Randal I would. I couldn't live on that stuff.

James And I shudder to think of that kitchen of yours, all those pieces of flesh, disguised as chops, steak and mince . . . but it's all flesh and what you eat is what you are.

Randal And I am flesh.

James All flesh is grass.

Randal You ought to look like grass, by that token . . . all green and sappy. Salads, day in, day out, summer and winter.

James Your blood would be much purer.

Randal Besides . . . think back . . . Chicken Marengo, jugged hare, game pie . . . I'd hate to work out how much flesh you've put away

145

in your time.

James I'm a reformed man. And my consolation, Randal – my expiation, is to think of all those innocent pigs, sheep, cows, grouse and deer, who are today running alive and gloriously free, whereas, because of my greed, they might now be dead.

Randal They are dead. Someone else has eaten them, that's all. You don't think your conversion to vegetarianism – one item in this ascetic package deal of yours, has cut much ice in the animal kingdom, do you?

James After all this time here, with me, you will see the new life as a passing fad, another of my indulgences – you still do not accept the truth. Where others indulge themselves by acquiring, I indulge by abstaining. They dress. I strip.

Randal Join a nudist colony.

James I catch cold too easily.

Randal Coward.

James I pay no attention to what I wear, you have to allow that.

Randal You make sure it's always black or grey. But think what you used to wear! The hand-made mohair suits, silk shirts, velvet opera cloaks, cravats . . .

James I am doing my penance. I do penance every time you leave the door ajar, and the smell of burning flesh drifts down the passage.

Randal You know why I have to go out occasionally, to mingle with the locals? Because conversation here is so bloody limited . . . round and round the garden, like a teddy-bear. (*The clock strikes*) Half an hour.

James Help me with my cross-word, exercise your faculties. 'Oh, what a noble mind is here . . .' Nine letters.

Randal You can stop that!

James My dear Randal, it's here . . . fourteen across, see for yourself, look. Besides, Diana does not have a 'noble mind', never did. And now, Diana does not have a mind at all. (*Pause*) Don't lose your temper.

Randal (*Icy*) I'll clear away.

James Please do, dirty dishes are offensive.

Randal *Life* is offensive.

(*Long pause*)

James Things were a little . . . hysterical. Earlier.

Randal Never mind. (*He puts dishes on a tray*)

James (*Casual*) Do you remember Jenny?

Randal (*Guarded*) Yes.

James Hmmm. Nice. Wore red rather a lot. Suited her. Not many women can carry it off. We all went to the last night of the Proms. I can't imagine why . . . and ended up, very drunk on warm champagne, lying about the garden. A hot night. Nights were always hot, then. The champagne was warm because Diana had forgotten to tell Mrs Moon to defrost the refrigerator, or Mrs Moon had failed to hear her . . . or something. Things were always disorganised. A full moon. I wore a frilled shirt. Ugh! (*Pause*) It surprised me, when you didn't marry Jenny.

Randal I'll go and organise your tea-tray.

James Women can really be terribly nice. Diana's hair. Red dresses. My experience has set no standard.

Randal Mrs Pringle brought up a cake this morning.

James There you are – women. How kind!

Randal I meant, would you like some with your tea?

James But not foreign women. The europeans run to fat and the Americans go scraggy. Buy British, Randal, I should. Or buy local, rolls in the Somerset hay – perhaps you do?

Randal Sometimes, you . . .

James Your nerves are on edge today.

Randal You haven't said whether you want cake or not. It's Madeira cake.

James I was an appalling husband, but you'd be rather a good one. Look at your accomplishments . . . you'd be considerate, help with bathing the children, thrifty . . . play fair in the quarrels, seeing both points of view. Tidy away your clothes neatly at night.

Randal If the boy scouts come ringing, ignore them, they've already mown the lawn – half of it – badly – one of them cut his toe, and then they touched me for fifty pence. Fifty! That's ten bob. Ten jobs, should have been.

James After all, you're thirty-eight, Randal, you'll be on the shelf before you can say knife, and you'll do no good stuck in this place.

Randal Don't start feeling sorry for yourself, because I will not, and do not, feel sorry for you. Not today.

James You can't marry *me*.

Randal It's bad enough that I have to go at all.

James She is your sister, and isn't blood thicker than water, Randal?

Get your priorities right, *I* am water.

Randal If the phone rings, say . . .

James You know perfectly well I never answer the telephone. We used to spend half our days on the telephone – or rather, Diana did, madly, wildly handing out invitations, for fear she and I would be left alone together.

Randal I shall have to stop for petrol, too. I'll be late.

James You? Impossible, you were a boy scout yourself.

(*Randal walks to the door*)

By the way . . . tell Diana that I want to divorce her . . . free myself entirely.

Randal You bloody sadist!

James Language! Not like you – a clergyman's son. Besides, bad language is so untidy.

Randal Bloody sadist . . . it's what you are. She, Diana, she's the one they're treating, the one they sent away. They've got the wrong person. It should be you.

James I wondered when we'd get around to that again.

Randal You're warped . . . criminal. Diana may be ill . . . terrified . . . Yes, she tries, she fights, but she is still terrified, of life, of herself, of everyone . . . but it's only you she needs to be afraid of.

James Oh, she used to be. Ask her.

Randal But she is not dangerous and not evil. She doesn't enjoy any of it, but you do. What has it done for you, this precious three years locked away in this house? This – 'purging', this inner voyage of discovery, this sack-cloth and ashes game? It's driven you mad. If you weren't mad already.

James You are repeating yourself. And upsetting yourself. You're hysterical. Calm down, Randal.

Randal You say you're 'searching for truth'. You?

James You will be late.

Randal 'Tell Diana I want to divorce her, to free myself entirely'.

James . . . if you have to buy petrol, or whatever it is. I'm not mechanical.

Randal I may not go at all.

James Wise, perhaps, in your present state.

Randal Telephone them and say you are preventing me from going.

James My dear Randal, how on earth can I prevent you? I have no power to prevent you from packing up and getting out altogether, leaving me to my own devices.

Randal You have no devices.

James There is the door. Pass through it.

Randal Only deceits . . .

James Oh no, deceits are over and past . . . and the voice of the turtle is heard in our land.

Randal And conceits. Evasions, lies, self-indulgences and treachery.

James I am more than capable of examining my own conscience and finding myself wanting, thank you. I have spent the past three years here doing so and left no stone unturned. And you find many a nasty thing under stones.

Randal A pose. A game.

James I make a journey towards truth.

Randal You wouldn't recognise the truth about anything . . . past or present, about me or yourself, this place, this life, *anything*.

James These bursts of hysteria are alarming. A family tendency. Always keep control.

Randal You live by fraud and fantasy.

James I think it's sex.

Randal What?

James Repression, or fear of failure or . . . something. Any normal man would have married her . . . Jenny. Any *normal* man. (*Pause*) You are going to hit me. You want to. But you will not. I've turned my back on you . . . see? You wouldn't shoot a man in the back, it's against your principles . . . or scruples. Well . . . (*He turns*) Here I am. Face to face. Come, strike me, I'm defenceless. Aha! No, you wouldn't. You wouldn't.

(*Long silence*)

Randal Will you want cake?

James No.

Randal Right.

James Oh, make the sun shine, Randal, then it would be . . . Does Diana look out and wait for the sun to shine?

Randal She . . . walks in the sun sometimes.

James Walks. Ah. Diana in the sun. We went to Tuscany and Diana walked in the sun there. Walked.

Randal If you . . . you could see the doctor again. Another doctor, they might . . .

James They won't. Bloody trick-cyclists.

Randal But he did say . . .

James I know what he said, they said, you said, we all fall *down*. If I tried to stand I should fall down. Do go, Randal.

Randal I must, yes. Now . . . money . . . car keys . . .

James You won't tell her . . . about the divorce.

Randal I never tell her anything. Have you got everything?

James Oh, I have got everything. I'm tired. I'm so tired. That's all.

Randal Water in the kettle, tea in the pot, only to switch on . . . Well . . . as usual.

James As usual.

Randal And don't forget about the boy scouts. I wouldn't put anything past them. They did give me a little sticker-thing to put on the window, only I seem to have lost it.

James No jobs for bobs, no bobs for jobs.

Randal No.

James I wanted to take her to bed . . . Jenny.

Randal I'm very late.

James Perhaps I *did*. I was capable of anything in those days.

Randal You might . . . send a message to Diana. It might . . .

James She'd none of it. And I have nothing to say. Oh, for Christ's sake, Randal, get it over with, get out, I can't stand this every week.

Randal I need a drink. I always seem to need a drink now, on . . .

James Don't say it.

Randal It's only a day of the week. And today, she may be . . . a little better . . . something . . . she . . .

James Get *out*!

(*Randal walks slowly out. Closes the door*)

So that I can begin to sit and . . . wait for you to come back.

(*Long silence. Then James sings*)

'Where have you been all the day? Randal, my son.

Where have you been all the day? My handsome young man.

I've been at the green-wood, Mother . . .

A-looking for my . . . brother.

Make my bed soon, for I am sick to my soul.

And I fain would lie down'.

(*Early that evening. James's room*)

(*A record of unaccompanied plainsong. It fades. The door opens. Pause*)

Diana James . . .

James What? (*Long pause*) What are you . . . I didn't hear the car, I heard no one come in . . . no one should come in here.

Diana (*Very anxious*) He . . . Randal . . . he said something about the village . . . the car . . . Yes, something needs doing to the car and . . . someone . . . a man. Sawyer? Yes . . . Sawyer, he said. He dropped me, and I walked up the drive. By myself. I haven't done that before. Been here . . . before. I haven't been out by myself for . . . It's very strange. Here. That great hill . . . mound . . . looming up behind the house, waiting to . . . pounce. And . . . it's very bare in here, not a bit as I imagined, not like the old house. It's . . . white walls, grey curtains, that bare wood and . . . you . . . grey. Is this how you live now?

    (*Silence*)

It was as if my head didn't belong to my body . . . walking up the drive. By myself. (*Pause*) We bought two bottles of wine, on the way . . . Oh, they must be in the car still. They gave us a plastic carrier bag . . . free, I mean, we didn't have to pay for it. We paid for the wine. Nice wine. It looked. Is there . . . Could I have a drink now? You see, the wine is still in the car and Randal . . . something at the garage. I told you that. Yes. It's just that I feel strange. Here. Could I have a drink? Do you have drinks, here?

    (*Silence*)

Well . . . I'll sit and wait for the wine. For Randal. You see, I might have come away weeks ago, they would have let me, they wanted me to try, but I couldn't pluck up courage. I wish you would say something. A word or . . . I wish you wouldn't look at me like that. Stare . . . I don't . . .

James (*Quiet. Incisive*) I cannot bear *colour*.

Diana Colour? There is no colour. None. It's like . . . like a cell. Like a prison. You know, there, in the hospital . . . it isn't the same, they have colour there, Oh, lots of it. Curtains – orange, lime green with big flowers and bold shapes, patterns and . . . I painted big coloured pictures, too. I wasn't very good. You'd have expected the walls to be mud or . . . the rooms to be like this. Grey. They're not. Primrose and bright yellow and blue . . . they make the best of it. And the flowerbeds . . . great strips of colour . . . geraniums and salvias and huge golden daisies, all together. (*Pause*) When I walked up this drive, by myself, it was all green, and then I came to the roses, such a lot of roses . . . but they are all white. Nice, but . . . if I lived here, do you know what I'd do, I'd employ some gardeners, dressed in sandwich boards like playing cards, to paint the roses red, you know, like . . .

James But you do not live here.

Diana I can't understand it . . . you, in this room, this . . .

James I have said that I cannot bear *colour*.

Diana Oh . . . my . . . my coat? My orange coat?

James I have to look away, the colour offends me.

Diana But we went to buy it, today, this afternoon, specially . . . I mean, it is a new coat, a . . . celebration, Randal and I chose it, it was expensive too . . . well, fairly. It's very fashionable, they said. I hadn't cared for such a long time . . . about clothes. When you remember how I used to . . . do you remember? I got excited . . . the shop, walking across soft carpets, swinging around rails of garments, coats, dresses, all hanging there, bright. It made my heart thud. (*Pause*) I'm sorry you don't like it.

James I cannot bear . . .

Diana Don't shout, please don't shout, I'm afraid of it, the shouting. A lot of them shouted, there. Perhaps I did, at first. There was an old man with no teeth, he shouted . . . they have drugs and . . . but it's what I remember, the worst of it, in the old days, you shouting at me, and that crying. The baby was always crying. (*Pause*) You'd rather I took my coat off? Yes. Perhaps I don't like it myself now. So much.

James Please don't put it there on the bed, I don't want to look at it.

Diana I . . . where? If I drop it on the floor, behind the chair? Is that all right? I don't know what you want. It's so strange . . . you and Randal, here. Nothing is like it used to be. He told me, but I didn't understand. Miles to the village, up the dark drive, and then this . . . grey house, and that mound . . . over there.

James Barrow. (*He wheels to the window*) Barrow – prehistoric burial place. Bodies. Cast-off selves. Treasure, too, jewels . . . and tools and weapons. They buried them with their dead . . . for the journey to the new life, I suppose. The Danes laid their dead Kings in ships and loaded them down with loot and launched them alone onto the deep, the crossing by water. It's all . . . journeying. (*Pause*) Sometimes, a hawk hovers over the barrow. But the sun has gone.

Diana I wish Randal would come back, I wish he would hurry. If I heard the car, I . . . We bought wine. I told you. I'm coherent now, only . . .

James He said nothing about a visit.

Diana Not . . . a visit.

James   You can't stay? Pity. The roses are blooming so nicely. But then, you don't like white roses.

Diana   I mean, I don't have to go back there, not at all. I was . . . I am better . . . it was only that, when I walked up that drive, by myself . . . Does the sun never shine into this room? That mound . . .

James   Barrow . . .

Diana   . . . blocks it out. Like a prison wall. I visited a prison once. When I woke up one morning in London, and you were out or away . . . it was the time when you were always out or away, I forget, I felt entirely frivolous in that place. I looked round me. Four-poster bed, drapes, full-length mirrors, thick rugs, those bright blue curtains, polished rosewood . . . all so expensive. I curled my toes up in the pile of the rug and then looked down at my feet on the marble tiles of the bathroom floor. I wrapped a towel round me and it was like a sheep's fleece. I felt worthless. Expendable. So . . . I visited a prison. I made all the arrangements, rang people up, bang, snap, Oh you know me . . . Knew me. I went with a social worker. Nice. Not as you'd expect. She was married, but quite young and . . . motherly . . . I felt ashamed. Of my clothes. She said nothing. It was so appalling. Grey, no sun, no colour, clean, but . . . And now here, and I feel ashamed of my expensive coat and . . . how do you stand it here? This isn't . . . *you*.

James   Oh, but it is me. Not the man you knew. But the real man.

Diana   It needs . . . Oh, singing and dancing . . . Where are all the dance records? Where is everything?

James   Stored. But what is mine is yours, I suppose, you can have whatever you want. The house is let, it brings in a surprising amount of money, and then, Randal has kept a few things. I never go into his rooms.

Diana   But there was always music – dance music, as well as, Oh, all that opera, and Chopin, and that was lovely, too. But there was so much music to dance to.

James   Not now. There is no dancing here.

Diana   I don't remember any of these records (*Looking*) Scarlatti . . . harpsichord . . . Bach cello sonatas . . . Bartók . . . plainsong. It's all so . . . bleak.

James   Austere. There is nothing superfluous.

Diana   Don't you remember what our mothers said . . . all the mothers and grandmothers . . .? 'Make your own entertainment, *we* had to'.

James It isn't a question of entertainment.

Diana But there might be something on the radio. (*She turns it on. A consort of viols. Flips programmes until she finds a dance band*) Oh, that tune, I remember, I loved that tune. I can dance to that! (*She hums*) It's all it needs here. Or . . . it's *something.* (*James snaps the radio off. Diana shouts*) Why don't you *dance*, for God's sake? (*Dead silence*) I'm sorry. (*Pause*) Do I . . . distress you?

James Distress . . .

Diana What is it?

James Diana in distress.

Diana No. I'm really . . . happy enough. I feel different. Clean. As if I'd been put into cold storage and then brought out again and . . . very slowly thawed. Restored. Ice-maiden . . . I used to be that. Heartless. But now it *beats.*

James I could make it beat. Thud-thud. Thud-thud. Faster.

Diana No. I'm not afraid of you now.

James I might distress you. I might . . . ask you for a divorce. I might say . . . don't you remember our child, who died? Oh, it doesn't distress me. Think, after all, it would have lived, grown up, among a million hazards . . . sharp blades, plunging lorries, faulty electric plugs, temptations to drink and drugs, diseases of the body. We all die, sooner or later, and the child sooner, in six inches of water. I should feel . . . distress. Weep. I have spent three years in this room, waiting. Nothing. A punishment, perhaps.

Diana A . . . discovery, perhaps.

James One of us must weep.

Diana I used to weep for you. If Randal would come back . . .

James . . . We should have two bottles of wine. He is not back. I rarely drink now. (*Pause*) Do you love your brother? Don't look startled. In the quest for truth, one needs to see things from all angles.

Diana Yes. I love my brother . . . of course.

James Not so. Many do not.

Diana I love my brother.

James You don't love me. You don't like me. I am not likeable. If you were to know me now . . . But then, the purpose of life is to 'know thyself'.

Diana And then, reach out, take the fruit from the tree. You forget that you have been here, voluntarily, and I have been there – involuntarily . . . at least, at first. Until it became very important for me to stay. I made myself . . . finish the course.

James Surprising. You never finished things. You were always taking up fancies . . . whims. Dress-making, left about the house in pieces. Home-made wine – awful bottles and jars, fermenting and putrefying in larders. When there was all the money in the world, for dress-shops and wine-merchants.

Diana I had to give myself something to do.

James Crochet, still on the needle. And then . . . children are so messy.

Diana I wanted to avoid my own thoughts.

James They catch up with one.

Diana Yes. I could have left the hospital . . . come away whenever I wanted. But then I should have been cheating, I should not have known. If *you*, knew *me*, now.

James And the moral of that is, 'Birds of a feather flock together, but one swallow doesn't make a summer'. The only slight problem is that the tenants have a lease on the London house until the end of this year, and I never break promises now. However, luckily there is plenty of money, as ever, you can take whatever you want out of storage and set up anywhere at all. No problem.

Diana Oh, you haven't changed!

James (*Angry*) I am entirely and utterly changed.

Diana And I . . . After the child died, I didn't cry. That was the beginning of it all, perhaps. In there, I talked and they talked, asked questions endlessly – it was like trying to syphon blood out of a collapsed vein, but they went on, dig-dig-dig. Cry, they said . . . I said . . . cry, feel distress, loss, guilt. Feel . . . normal human misery. Cry. I cried. At myself, in anger and despair, and sometimes, at you. For you. I cried at birds with damaged wings and flowers wilting in jam jars for lack of water, and because Sam couldn't dance, and at a broken brick in the wall and famine in the East, and at an old man with no teeth and no visitors, at bombs on the television and lung-cancer statistics. But not about the child, that death, that six inches of water.

James Never? Never?

Diana One day, I was shaping a pot – I became rather good at pottery. Odd. I was never any good with my hands. It took me two school terms to make a shoe-bag. I don't understand why I ever bothered to try all that dress-making.

James Pottery – slimey, wet clay, all over your hands, drying into crumbs and flaking off. *Messy.*

Diana It was a good pot . . . clean . . . even beautiful. It's new, the pottery room there, whitewashed brick with geraniums on the windowledges. The sun shone in. It fell onto my hands. I looked down at my hands. I smashed my hands down onto the pot and it splattered everywhere, and I bruised my hands, quite badly. I cried. All day and all night, cried for hours. I cried for him, out of love, for that birth and life and death. I cried for the child then.

James Then . . . all is well with you. For you, it's all over. The light at the end of the tunnel.

Diana But here – there is no light.

James Perhaps the sun never shone. I imagined it.

Diana We went to Tuscany and the sun shone. That was a beautiful place.

James Olive trees and vines and the brick-red earth.

Diana I should like to go there, and just sit. Breathe. Sit in the sun.

James Then go. You are perfectly free.

Diana But would it have changed?

James All things have changed.

Diana I still don't understand why you are *here*. Why you like it.

James Does it seem to you that I *like* it?

Diana Then . . . go. You are perfectly free.

James Not so.

Diana There are no locks.

James I have to stay here, until . . . the sun shines and I achieve my moment of grief and hour of distress and cry . . . not only for myself. This is my . . . pottery room.

Diana But if you're so unhappy . . .

James Isn't that why I have to stay?

Diana How . . . unnatural. Unlike you.

James I am – unlike me.

Diana Self-torment . . . why not buy yourself a hair shirt and be done. Or else . . . enjoy yourself.

James Do you?

Diana Enjoy?

James Making pots and choosing bright new coats, walking in the gardens. Waking and sleeping.

Diana I am . . . learning to enjoy myself, yes. It seems hard. And then, suddenly . . . not hard at all.

James Oh, to enjoy yourself, and to know it at the moment of enjoyment is the hardest thing in the world. Suffering is easy enough, but if you achieve the other . . . Well, I envy you, Diana. You should go to Tuscany.

Diana While you stay here, punish yourself, or whatever it is. But why subject someone else to it? Randal . . .

James Is also 'perfectly free'.

Diana I wish he would come back. I feel so . . . uneasy. Talking to you. Being with you again.

James Randal may not come back at all. The car . . . Sawyer . . . all an excuse? Perhaps he has cut and run with two bottles of wine in a free plastic carrier bag. But I don't think you need worry. Randal is happy here, Randal has an easy capacity for enjoyment. He drinks home-brewed cider with the locals.

Diana He looks after you. He's everything . . . cook, cleaner, companion, nurse . . . why?

James Randal is *not* my nurse. I require . . . some help, but I am not ill.

Diana A man who is well can walk.

James But not all men who can walk are well. One morning, the sun may shine and then I may walk.

Diana I'm afraid of you again.

James Go outside, take the air. You don't have to sit with me. Or stay here at all.

Diana He'll bring the wine. Then it may be better . . . after some wine.

James There would be wine in Tuscany, you would drink it, sitting in the sun.

Diana Why are you so anxious for me to go away?

James Wouldn't it be more remarkable if I wanted you to stay here?

Diana I can't go outside . . . that mound . . . barrow . . . terrifies me, too. I could run back, back there, to the flowerbeds, to the pottery room with the sun shining in and geraniums on the window-ledge.

James To the shouting of an old man with no teeth and no visitors. To distress?

Diana (*Despair*) Then where can I go? There is . . . nowhere.

James Not here, certainly.

Diana This is a terrible place.

James Yes.

157

Diana I wish I knew . . . someone. I wish I knew myself, even.

James You know your brother.

Diana Where *is* my brother?

    (*Diana begins to cry quietly. The sound of a car*)

James Here is your brother.

      (*The following afternoon*)

Diana If I sit here and look at you, if you just go on talking to me, it isn't so bad. Though I know he is there, and if I go to the window, I see him. He's very still, and he has his back to the house. But even the sight of his back terrifies me. And that barrow. (*Pause*) We went to Switzerland once.

Randal The year after you were married, yes.

Diana We went on the train. I woke up and it was just dawn. The train had stopped. I rolled up the blind of the sleeping car, and there was a village. Little houses with red roofs, like toy houses, all clustered at the foot of a great, black mountain. It was so high and so huge, I thought it was going to topple over and fall . . . on the houses, on the train. On me. I was terrified. James laughed. (*Pause*) Talk to me, Randal.

Randal Remember . . . wet Saturday afternoons at the Rectory? We used to play Racing Demon and Beggar my neighbour and Strip Jack Naked. Illicitly. Card games were wicked. Think how much secret pleasure we would have missed in an ordinary household.

Diana I suppose it wasn't really an ordinary household. Though we were quite ordinary children.

Randal Children are never ordinary.

Diana Father should have married young. Had his children earlier in life.

Randal I'm surprised father ever married at all. But perhaps he was thinking of company in his old age.

Diana Was he happy?

Randal Mother was happy. Love makes a good many miseries endurable.

Diana Then I was never in love.

Randal Love compromises, too. Father would never compromise.

Diana James did not. Does not.

Randal So he would have it appear.

Diana And – appearances are deceptive? Yes.

Randal Very.

Diana While you were taking him out into the garden, I looked along his bookshelf. I wanted entertainment.

Randal Oh, we have no entertainment here!

Diana Those awful books . . . essays, sermons, dictionaries. No pictures or conversations . . .

Both together 'And what is the use of a book without pictures or conversations?'

Diana Oh, when I look at you, when you talk, I remember so many things. I miss so many things. Not from that life with him. From *our* life. I should like to take all those books into the garden and make a bonfire and burn them before his eyes. The flames would leap. They would terrify him.

Randal But he rarely reads.

Diana What *does* he do here?

Randal Sits. Thinks. Sleeps. Talks to me about his new-found self, and the voyage of inner discovery, denounces the past and all pleasure. Baits me.

Diana And you let him.

Randal It rolls off my back, mostly.

Diana Oh, it is *not* like father. I've blamed father for too much. He believed in enjoyment, Randal – all right, unsophisticated pleasures . . . naive, some people would say. Family games, the garden, walks. And swimming. Do you remember how much pleasure it gave him, teaching us to swim?

Randal But we wanted forbidden fruits. Games of cards and Consequences, played in church under cover of hymn books. Later on – oh, late nights and drink and dancing. Unsuitable company!

Diana Extravagance. Sins. Though they were not. Not to God.

Randal But to father.

Diana When I first arrrived in London, I said nothing, I only looked and listened, trying to learn the secrets. I wanted to belong.

Randal 'The inner ring.'

Diana Yes, and to enter it, it seemed that first, you had to lay claim to an unhappy childhood. And so I did. I wanted one for myself, and soon, they believed in it, and so did I. But *were* we unhappy? I no longer know what was true for us at the time. I remember picnics and stealing from the raspberry canes, I remember putting one of father's dog-collars around the neck of a snow-man.

Randal I remember dressing up as the White Rabbit, wearing a pair of mother's best gloves!

Diana On wet Saturday afternoons, we sometimes made toffee. But it always turned to fudge.

Randal Oh, I remember the fudge!

Diana Yes, I think we were happy. Are you happy now?

Randal I never stop to ask myself. I'm simply . . . here.

Diana You can't be happy, no one could be, here, unhappiness is a condition of this appalling place. *His* condition. Unhappiness was what James has always required. In others.

Randal And now, in himself.

Diana Yet this room does seem more comfortable. Just a little. We've made it untidy – wine bottles on the table. Coffee cups strewn about.

Randal He dislikes untidiness.

Diana He's a hypocrite. He frightens me. This house frightens me. But they can't touch me, Randal, not now. I can run away He may try to hold me with his glittering eye, but I can turn my back. Not you, though . . . you are in *thrall*.

Randal No. I am needed. And . . . I've nothing else to do with my life, it isn't an especially valuable commodity.

Diana Suppose that I need you – more than he does? What then?

Randal Do you?

Diana Once, when we were children, you went away for two weeks to. stay with a friend in Wales. I was nine. I couldn't bear it.

Randal I rode a pony in Wales. It clambered to the top of a mountain . . . or what seemed like a mountain . . . the roof of the world. I thought I might fly! I was happy then.

Diana When the child was born, you saw it first. Before James. It seemed to me that it really belonged to you, and not to him at all. Is that a wicked thing to say?

Randal Not wicked. I don't think you . . . understand what it means.

Diana I understand very little. Now. But I've got time to learn. Where should I go, Randal? I should like to go back – to the Rectory garden. But nothing would be the same. Where should I go? You see – no answer, because there *is* no answer. So – I must invent a place, take up a map and close my eyes and point a finger, and where my finger rests, there I shall go. Or to Tuscany. But that may have changed too, and then I should lose myself again, and my hold is always precarious.

Randal I went back to the Rectory. I drove the car very slowly down the village street and parked beside the church wall. My hands were sweating. I wondered what I should find.

Diana Oh, tell me!

Randal I walked around the church and down the path.

Diana The back path . . . the private path.

Randal I stood under the apple trees at the bottom of the garden and looked towards the house.

Diana The apple trees were tall – as tall as the house.

Randal Now – they seem to have shrunken down into themselves, like very old men.

Diana The day you fell out of the apple tree . . .

Randal If I hadn't broken my arm, I should have been beaten for climbing. You came into my bedroom that night. You said, 'It is a punishment' – touching the plaster. I knew it.

Diana The raspberry canes?

Randal Still there.

Diana The swing?

Randal No. Not the swing.

Diana But then, a swing would scarcely last – out in all weathers, thirty years or more. Wood rots, rope disintegrates. When I was in the swing and you were in the tree . . . Oh, it all comes back. We *were* happy then.

Randal The Rectory was empty.

Diana Then we could go back, we could live there. I could look after you, and we would plant hundreds of marvellous, bright flowers.

Randal No.

Diana And we would leave James out, to rot like the swing, leave him where he is, in his wheelchair and he would disintegrate in the end. (*Silence*)

What is he looking at? What is he thinking? Oh, I would paint those white roses. They are everything I hate – snow and swans and ghosts and wedding veils and virginal sheets. And winding sheets. In London, we had cyclamen silk curtains and walls the colour of indigo and two fans made of peacock feathers splayed out on either side of a gilded mirror. We had dressing gowns of emerald green. And *he* chose them. So much extravagance and show. So much pleasure.

Randal But in the end, there was no pleasure.

Diana There were people, things to do. I was always singing or dancing or laughing.

Randal Or crying.

Diana We were *alive*. He was alive then. Dear God! That barrow is a burial place, and where does the barrow stop and this house begin, where is the difference?

Oh, I want some wine, a river of wine! What's wrong with you? Can't you enjoy yourself any more either, are you buried? I don't care about anyone else. When the child died, I stopped loving it, because there was nothing there *to* love. But you . . . you must not . . . You have. You have sold your soul to the devil.

Randal James isn't the devil. Only an unhappy man.

Diana You don't know the half of it!

Randal I'll go down to the village and buy some wine for you.

Diana No. If you went, I should be afraid again.

Randal Come with me then.

Diana 'Come fly with me, come fly, let's fly. . .' We could, we could!

Randal But I mustn't be long, I have to make his tea.

Diana 'Have to make his tea.' You will go to your grave making his tea, and be buried in that barrow.

Randal I wish you would stop talking about the barrow.

Diana Why? Because you're afraid of it, too? But you never used to be afraid of anything. You climbed to the top of the elm tree. You climbed down the drainpipe at midnight. You won a shilling when the grocer's boy dared you to walk across Hender's field while the bull was in there loose, and you stole a cigarette from Mrs Dodds and smoked it in the tool-shed on a Sunday. I was always afraid, the air of the whole house was thick with danger, when I breathed it in my bladder went weak with fear.

The air here has the same smell. When James asked me to marry him, I was too afraid to refuse, though I knew that acceptance would mean fear for the rest of my life. And when the child died, I felt faint with relief, because I should no longer have to fear for it, night and day. I don't want to sit in this room and talk and talk, about James and the barrow and the dead child and how afraid I have always been.

Randal We could play cards.

Diana Anything.

Randal Or some music.

Diana There is no music. Only sounds that scrape and wail slow wails, or clatter together like bones. Even father liked music!

Randal Rousing hymns and brass bands.

Diana In the hospital, there was a dance every Friday night. 'The Valeta' and the 'Military Twostep' and the 'Gay Gordons'. Old men shuffled about and women with blank eyes and mouths that twitched, tried to keep time, and all night long, Mrs Reilly sang 'Lilli Marlene', over and over again, sitting in the corner where the pipes of the radiator joined. Whenever the music stopped you heard it. 'Lilli Marlene'. One Friday night, there was a fight, because Sam ... Sam who had fits – brought in a chisel, concealed it down his trousers, a chisel from the woodwork shop. And who let *Sam* go into the woodwork shop? He had odd eyes, one green, one blue and they lit up like the eyes of a jackdaw at the sight of metal – bright blades. Sam attacked Mrs Reilly with the chisel, it took three male nurses and a doctor with a hypodermic to move him. People screamed. Or just stared. And Mrs Reilly went on singing 'Lilli Marlene'. But it was something. The dance. People did try to enjoy themselves. There was music. I saw father weeping, once, because of some music. Mrs Dodd, had the radio on, and a band played 'Goodbye, Dolly Grey's Father stood in the passage outside the kitchen and wept.

Randal That's a song to make any man weep.

Diana (*Softly*) '... for I can no longer stay.
Hark, I hear the bugle calling.
Goodbye, Dolly Grey.'
He didn't see me. He wiped his eyes with a handkerchief and stood still. Listening. I felt ashamed to have spied on him. I went away. I loved father. (*Pause*) James can't weep.

Randal James does weep.

Diana For what? Himself? Does he tell you? Do you have secrets, Randal? We had secrets, you and I.

Randal Do you want to play cards?

Diana Every Thursday, you came to see me. I went to bed the night before and could never sleep, because tomorrow, you would come and then, I should not be afraid.

Randal I play clock patience sometimes. In my own room. It passes the time – some forms of patience are really quite complicated.

Diana I don't want to play *cards*. (*She sweeps them off the table*) No, leave them, let them lie there, scattered about anyhow. *Messy*. (*Pause*) This is not a good world, Randal.

Randal Perhaps you ought to ... rest.

Diana Is that the sort of thing my brother Randal would ever say? You *cluck*. Old woman.

Randal I really ought to make the tea.

163

Diana For James. And go to see if it's getting too cold out there, for James. Take a rug, take comfort, cluck-cluck for James. (*Pause*) *We* could have tea. Soft boiled eggs and buttered toast fingers and dunk them into the golden yolks, with very sweet tea out of blue and white mugs. Then we could sit on the floor and play an illicit game of cards. Cards are wicked. In *Great Expectations*, Pip plays cards with Stella, and she is angry, because he is ignorant, he calls a Jack Jack, but she calls it knave. How could you have a game called 'Strip Knave Naked'? James is Jack, stripped naked – *he* thinks. Pared to the white bone. But Jack is a knave, and it was a small boy who spoke the truth about the Emperor's new clothes. All right, come, play with me, Randal, sit on the floor with me here. Ace is four, King is three, Queen is two, Jack is . . . you remember. (*Pause*)
Once, we hid under the plush table cloth in the dining-room, and heard father come in, looking for something, and swear because he couldn't find it. He said, 'Damn it all' and we clutched one another's hands and hardly dared to breathe. But my hand trembled, the palm was sweating, and your hand was steady and cool. You. Never afraid. I should have liked to stay under that table forever. Or sit here. Listen . . . here is safe . . . and also . . . very dangerous. Here is . . . Ace . . . King . . . Queen . . . Jack. (*Silence*)

Randal I must bring James in.

Diana Wheel James in, like a guy, set him on high, for all to see. And then . . . *burn* him down!

Randal You should . . . .

Diana Tell me what I should do.

Randal Rest in your room.

Diana It is not *my* room.

Randal Please. Let me do what I have to. It's hard enough . . . I can manage, but not . . . you as well.

Diana Speak the truth, Randal. We had secrets, and we also had the truth. Say, 'Go away from here, Diana, from where you do not belong and are not wanted, go down the drive by yourself. Leave us.' You used to tell me what to do. Always.

Randal It is so *hard*.

Diana Poor Randal. Do you weep, too? Poor everyone. Poor James, even. But in Tuscany, I could drink wine, sitting in the sun and I should never weep. (*Pause*) Help me up. Hold me. Look. Poor

King. Queen. Jack. Card people. Let me touch your face. (*Pause*) There. Go out to him. It looks so cold.

(*A few minutes later*)

James I closed my eyes. I thought, I shall wait . . . count up to ten or twenty . . . and when I open my eyes, the clouds will have parted. The sun will shine. But . . . nothing. The clouds billowed about me like cold breath. It *was* cold.

Randal I'm sorry, I should have come out for you sooner.

James You were talking. I turned my head once and saw you through the window. Diana, sitting on the bed. You were too busy . . . remembering things? Yes. Familiar secrets. Where is she?

Randal Gone to rest – I think.

James It was very quiet out there. I waited for something to happen – for the barrow to burst open and the dead to rise up, fire and thunder. Or the sun. Nothing. Diana deserves to rest. I'm glad she can. But there should have been some . . . revelation. Well – we might all have tea together. Happy families! Tea and hot buttered buns and jam and cake. Do you remember Diana's parties? They all came then, from the highways and by-ways, the hedgerows and the ditches, lured in by the fairy-lights and the false laughter.

Randal At the Rectory, people were always coming in for tea. Parish-ioners with problems, lonely passers-by, flower-arrangers. Father thought a great deal of tea-time – the shared meal.

James Are you like him?

Randal No.

James Nor Diana?

Randal We are only like ourselves – we might have sprung from nowhere.

James If only one could. But at least one can choose where to set oneself down and take root. I chose. So have you. Did she?

Randal Other people chose for her, I think. Now – she may be able to decide for herself. Where to be.

James But not here.

Randal She would never want to stay here.

James But I must. Oh, what if the sun never shines again, Randal? Or if you go, and Diana goes. I stay. Time staggers by, and fails and picks up again, and wanders on. While I wait. Watch and pray. Anything may happen. Or . . . nothing at all.

Randal Tea will happen.

James You comfort me. But the chair covers are crumpled, there is cigarette ash on the floor and empty wine-bottles clutter the table. Diana is here.

Randal Try to . . . treat her gently.

James She is a stranger and I was never any good with strangers. You might teach me. (*Pause*) Why are those cards scattered about the floor?

Randal We might have played a game. Passed the time.

James Like children. You tried to teach me a card game once.

Randal Canasta.

James You always beat me. I'm a bad learner.

Randal Because you wouldn't try.

James What was it you said? I was like the boy who . . . yes, who said, 'I'll take my bat home, and *then* you'll be sorry.' (*Pause*) I should like some treacle on toast. That used to be a treat! Sunday tea and treacle. My mother's hand, holding the toast on a fork in front of the fire. Her rings *blazed*. I loved her then.

Randal If we have any treacle.

James And call Diana – we'll be cosy. We three.

Randal She may not . . .

James Want to be cosy, with me? No.

Randal It's only that she finds it very strange here. So different. It was a shock, I suppose.

James A shock for me, when she walked in.

Randal I should have told you. I know.

James Pray for your sister, Randal. She has no place in this world.

Randal She may go to Tuscany.

James We conceived the child in Tuscany, and that was the greatest evil ever done. But when I went to the nursing home, after it was born . . . when I stood over that curious, institutional cot and looked down . . . that was a shock. That was – strange. I had no idea what would happen to me.

Randal And what happened?

James Something . . . I've never spoken about. To anyone. A secret I never told. I was thinking about it, out there in the garden just now.

Randal You loved the child?

James No. Worse. I looked down and saw that – *it loved me*. It was making a sound. A whimper . . . something. And then it was quite silent. Eyes open. Eyes that looked at me. Looked and saw . . . a blur, I suppose, some dark, shadowy, mysterious figure. But *my* eyes were clear. And I saw love. It never happened again.

(*During the last speech Diana has come in*)

Diana (*From the doorway*) There was no need for it to happen again.

Randal I thought you were resting . . .

Diana I was packing my bag.

James Go and make the tea, Randal. We need . . . comfort.

(*Randal goes. Closes the door. Diana comes down the room*)

James That bright coat . . .

Diana It is the only one I have and I should be cold without it.

James I can look at it now. It seems almost . . . familiar. Things have changed since you came yesterday. But you will stay to tea? What a curious invitation from a man to his wife!

Diana Appropriate. This is not my house.

James Is it mine now? I wonder. I look at it through your eyes, and through Randal's. It does seem . . . strange. I even begin to wonder why I came here. What I hoped to achieve.

Diana Distress.

James In recompense for love? A moment of love I did not deserve, did not achieve after a struggle . . . it was simply – *given*.

Diana Is love ever – deserved?

James Or won? Or gambled for? I don't know, Diana. The more you think you know . . . the more the outlines become . . . blurred. Perhaps I shall find out.

Diana Perhaps I shall.

James Oh, but you have.

Diana No. I want to go a long way. Take a train. I love trains. Standing on remote stations, late at night, watching trains rush by, seeing the lighted windows . . . capsules . . . people caught in a second of eating or drinking or sleeping. I love waiting for trains. The smell of them, and the sound of the wheels . . . And then . . . a boat, and the boat will lurch this way and that, and I shall lurch with it, towards some new world. Or some old world.

James And 'cry no more, lady, cry no more.'

Diana 'Men were deceivers ever.'

James Some. Well, I shall cry, in the end. And then – perhaps I shall walk again. And then . . . find a place.

Diana What are places?

James Rooms to cry in.

Diana And when you have cried?

James I daren't think so far ahead. Today, I have been thinking *back*. Pieces detach themselves from the past . . . memories . . . they're important. I stitch them together. I may make a coat of many colours. It will keep out the cold, at least. A bright coat. Sit down, please. Wait for the tea. For Randal. (*Pause*) Randal loves you.

Diana Loves *you*.

James Take him with you. You might be so lonely, sitting in Tuscany in the sun. I wish the sun would shine here. Just once. Just for a moment. (*He wheels to the window*) Look at it. Grey, grey and grey. But . . . there's the hawk – isn't it? I can't tell. Randal would know. A crow, probably – some dull bird. No . . . it *is* the hawk. I should like to hover in the air . . . high up . . . like a kite on an invisible string. Children come sometimes . . . stand on top of the barrow and fly kites. (*The door closes quietly*) They don't come often, but . . . Look. (*Pause*) Diana? Ah. (*Pause*) You could have stayed for tea. For the comfort of it, or . . . No one will follow you, you will walk down the long drive by yourself. So . . . I may walk. Why not? Try anything, we used to say . . . then. (*He begins to struggle out of his chair*) Then . . . I . . . shall . . . try . . . One hand on the . . . table . . . one hand on the arm of . . . this . . . chair. Wait . . . take a breath . . . strange . . . Then . . . then . . . stand . . . I am standing! Holding on, but . . . Oh, if you had stayed, look what you would have seen . . . signs and wonders . . . a fine thing . . . Then, I . . . let go this hand . . . let . . . go . . . that hand . . . then . . . I move a foot . . . a leg . . . I . . . move. Children must learn to walk. They *do* learn . . . the ground is steady beneath my feet . . . the ground is . . . I move the other foot and . . . I . . . (*He crashes to the floor. Screams in panic. Silence*) I . . . lie . . . On the ground. I can't . . . (*Pause. He calls out*) Randal! Randal . . . Oh God, Randal . . . help, help me, help me. Dear God . . . Randal . . .

   (*The door opens. Randal comes running in*)

Randal All right, I'm here. It's all right.

James I stood up. I . . .

Randal You fell . . . All right . . . here . . . keep still . . . let me move you . . .

James Help me . . .

Randal I am. Let your arms go . . . there . . . all right . . . you're not hurt. (*James is gasping*) . . . there. Rest in your chair . . .

James Diana *walked* . . . down the drive.

Randal I know.

James I wanted . . . something . . . something to hope for, or . . . like Diana.

Randal There is always something to hope for.

James But not *happiness*.

Randal Yes. Even that.

James Where? How?

Randal I think . . . you look in the opposite direction . . . into the distance, and then . . . it may steal up behind you.

James If it did . . . I should never dare to turn round . . . catch its eye, I shouldn't trust it, I should be afraid it was only a shadow.

Randal Oh, there are always shadows. Except in Paradise. Figures cast no shadows there.

James If I were to turn round and look out of that window . . . I might see . . . tell me what I might see.

Randal No. Turn around. Look for yourself. Take the chance.

James (*Long pause. Then he turns round*) The clouds have lifted . . . a little. A slivver of sunlight, lying across the garden . . . just touching the roses. The sun on the roses. It's late, isn't it? Past tea-time. Almost evening. The mist is still there . . . the sun won't last. It never lasts. There are the shadows, seeping and spreading. But not . . . black shadows, not . . . hopeless. The shadows are the colour of . . . violets.

Randal They often are.

James And I have never noticed.

Randal No.

James I couldn't bear to recognise any colour at all. It will be night. But then . . . there may be the moon and the other stars. And then . . . there will be tomorrow. Shall I be able to bear tomorrow?

Randal I don't know.

James I wanted you to know everything. (*Pause*) I'm very tired. The sun has gone. The roses are white again. The ghosts of roses. Dead. (*Pause*) Death is easy, Randal. Dying is easy. Sitting still among the shadows is easy. But Diana has gone into the sun, wearing a bright coat. Diana wept. So now . . . she will live. That is the hardest thing of all. And I must do it. I must.

Randal Yes.

James Begin . . . where do I begin?

Randal Only you can say.

James Then ... tomorrow. Tomorrow, I must begin to ... to *paint the roses*!